10 RULES to BREAK & 10 RULES to MAKE

The Do's And Don'ts For Designing Your Destiny

Bill Quain, Ph.D.

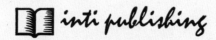 inti publishing

10 RULES TO BREAK
&
10 RULES TO MAKE
The Do's and Don'ts for Designing Your Destiny

By Bill Quain

Book cover by Cherry Design

Dedication

This book is dedicated to two special friends, Barry and Donna Render. It was Barry who first introduced me to the joys of writing books. Both Barry and Donna have been cheerleaders of *10 Rules to Break & 10 Rules to Make* from its very inception. This one's for you, Barry and Donna!

Acknowledgments

There are many people who helped make this book a reality. Without them, it would have been impossible to start this task, let alone complete it. It is my pleasure to thank them here.

After the initial idea for the book was hatched, the next step was to come up with a list of rules to "Break & Make." My special thanks to the following people for their contributions: Peter and Jeannine Norris, Maliz DePaul, Jim and Susan Higgins, Bob Ashley, Barry and Donna Render, my wife, Jeanne Quain, and my parents, Kay and Bill Quain, who also found the quotes for the beginning of each chapter.

This book has undergone many rewrites. Each reviewer left a special mark and provided a unique perspective in the editing process. Special thanks are due to the gang at INTI Publishing: Burke Hedges, Steve Price, and Katherine Glover. They led by example, and the manuscript is much better after their patient coaching and guidance.

Only a few authors are fortunate enough to have editors in their family. My wife, Jeanne Quain, and my mother, Kay Quain, worked on the manuscript from the very first draft. Jeanne had a double burden—caring for a husband/author while supervising the never-ending task of whipping this book into shape. Thank you.

Michael Thomas used heroic efforts to assemble my original manuscript. Neil Wasmund helped organize the chapters. Cherry Design, Inc. did a beautiful job on the cover design. And special thanks to Don Lee, who had the challenge of proofreading.

Susan Novotny worked some miracles on the interior design and layout. Thanks, Susan, the book looks great!

Finally, my special thanks to my two daughters, Amanda and Kathleen. They helped me understand that rules don't always make sense. When I tell them to "Calm down!" Amanda reminds me that excitement should be encouraged—in all of us.

Table of Contents

Introduction

Designing Your Destiny

Introduction

Designing Your Destiny

Even when laws have been written down, they ought not always to remain unaltered.

—Aristotle

It was one of those perfect summer days.

My wife, Jeanne, was pregnant with our second daughter, Kathleen. We were enjoying an early dinner with our older daughter, Amanda, at a table overlooking the intra-coastal waterway in Fort Lauderdale, Florida. You have to understand, I LOVE that stretch of water. In fact, I love almost ANY stretch of water, but that stretch in particular.

The sun was low, just starting to set. The heat of the day was beginning to give way to a more reasonable warmth that ever so slowly melted the ice in our glasses. Amanda was dozing off in the stroller, freeing Jeanne and me to enjoy our conversation.

I was feeling proud of myself. After all, I had just taken my family for a two-day visit to one of the great resort towns of the world! Now, we were relaxed, satisfied, and smug.

Then, it happened. My peaceful, secure, comfortable, and self-satisfied world was about to change—forever!

The sun disappeared as a huge shadow fell across our table. I looked up, and then I saw it. It wasn't a boat. It was a yacht. Like a messenger from my subconscious, it slowly cruised by my little corner of the world. It was so close that I could see every detail of the yacht, even with my poor eyesight.

It took a long time for that yacht to pass. And it peeled away my self-satisfaction as it went. As the stern of the yacht pulled even with our table, I saw a group of passengers on board, laughing and smiling. They looked like they were having so much fun that I almost laughed out loud myself. In that moment, it dawned on me.

These people were living by different rules.

Forgotten Dreams

Jeanne saw the expression on my face and held my hand. "What is it?" she asked. "What's the matter?"

"I had forgotten my dream," I said. "All these years, I have been going to school, getting my degrees, and teaching at universities. I have been working so hard on books, speaking engagements, and teaching. Yet, I am quite sure that none of the people on that boat—at least not the owner—are college professors. I had forgotten that there is a lot of money in the world, and there is absolutely no reason why WE shouldn't have more of it."

We talked late into the night. That incident on July 7, 1993, changed both of us. We made a decision that night. We decided to take a new, more realistic look at the way we lived, the goals we set, and the actions we were willing to take to get what we wanted.

My friends, that day Jeanne and I made a commitment to get our dream together. We made some hard choices—deciding to do some things we didn't necessarily want to do so that we could have the things we wanted for our family. We made plans to create an income stream and a lifestyle that would enable us to realize our dreams. In short, we began to *design our destiny.*

Why I Wrote This Book

Jeanne and I have experienced tremendous changes in our lives since that fateful day. Because we took time to renew our dreams and set our goals, we've been able to accomplish much more with our lives. We're no longer satisfied being members of the crew, taking orders, depending on someone else to set our course and control our fate. Today, I'm proud to say, we're captains of our own ship.

That's why I wrote this book. I wanted to help you design your own destiny by pointing out the "channel markers"—or rules—that will empower you to chart your own course through life. You may have to create some new rules for yourself...and challenge some old ones!

Challenge The Rules...And Rule Your Challenges!

I learned about challenging the rules at a very early age. When I was about 14, I began to lose my eyesight to a disease called macular degeneration. Today, I am legally blind. I am unable to drive a car, read print, or see the smiles of my children if they are more than a few feet away.

Imagine wearing a pair of glasses that has a thin film of petroleum jelly on the lenses. Now, tape a piece of black paper to the middle of each lens. The only vision you have is around the edges. That's what I see.

In order to overcome the physical limitations imposed by my handicap, I have learned to challenge the rules. I could have used my handicap as an excuse to limit my achievements, but that is not my style. I decided early in life to set my own rules so I could accomplish what I wanted out of life, not what others thought I should settle for.

What about you? What challenges do YOU have? Everyone has some handicap they need to overcome. You may be shy. You may lack self-confidence. You may come from a broken home. Or, you may simply be broke. All too often, these handicaps interfere with our dreams.

Whatever the challenge, you will never get anywhere by simply ACCEPTING the rules that others impose on you. If you want to design your own destiny, you will have to challenge some old rules, and create new ones.

More About This Book

I've divided the rules you'll be reading about into two categories—*10 Rules to Break* and *10 Rules to Make.* Let's take a brief look at what you'll learn in each category:

10 RULES to BREAK

In the first half of this book, I'm encouraging you to break 10 commonly held rules that all of us have heard, or said, all of our lives. These old clichés or rules may have been useful and valid in the past, but they don't hold up anymore. In fact, the *10 Rules to Break* hold us back.

For example, 500 years ago Columbus was wise enough to challenge the commonly held rule that the world was flat. Because he had the courage to challenge that rule, Columbus changed the course of the entire world. Likewise, in order for us to change our own course and design our own destiny, we MUST break these 10 rules, starting right now!

10 RULES to MAKE

The *10 Rules to Make*, on the other hand, are timeless! They will never go out of fashion. Like the Ten Commandments in the Bible, *10 Rules to Make* are immutable, universal laws.

These rules hold true across all cultures and for all time. Everyone must follow these rules or risk failure, just as a captain who ignores channel markers and lighthouse signals risks running his ship onto rocky shores.

Setting Sail

Designing your destiny will not be easy. You'll need to make some sacrifices. You'll need discipline. And yes, you'll need courage.

But once you set sail and you're charting your own course, you'll know firsthand the feeling of FREEDOM!

The freedom to make your own way in the world.

The freedom to captain your own ship.

Most of all, the freedom to seek a life of abundance, instead of settling for a life of compromise.

So as you read this book, examine the rules you are currently living your life by. Then carefully choose the rules that will empower you to *design your destiny*.

SECTION 1

10 RULES to BREAK

10 RULES to BREAK

Rule 1   *"Don't Waste Your Time with Dreams"*

Rule 2   *"The Best Things in Life Are Free"*

Rule 3   *"You're Too Young to Retire"*

Rule 4   *"Don't Rock the Boat"*

Rule 5   *"Build a Better Mousetrap and the World Will Beat a Path to Your Door"*

Rule 6   *"You Can't Be in Two Places at the Same Time"*

Rule 7   *"Hard Work Is Its Own Reward"*

Rule 8   *"Offer Constructive Criticism"*

Rule 9   *"Accept Only Valid Excuses"*

Rule 10   *"Don't Mix Business with Pleasure"*

10 RULES to BREAK

Overview

Intelligent Disobedience

The purpose of the *10 Rules to Break* section of this book is to help you change the way you view some outdated cliches, myths, and rules. But don't take my word for it. I want you to evaluate the "rules" placed before you, and consider whether or not they make sense FOR YOU as you design your destiny.

In other words, I'm challenging you to become "intelligently disobedient." I did not coin this phrase. "Intelligent disobedience" comes from the training program for Seeing Eye Dogs. These dogs guide blind people through their daily lives.

During their training process, two types of dogs are eliminated. The dogs that are unable to obey their masters are obviously dropped. And any dog that ONLY obeys the rules, without regard to changing circumstances, is dropped from the program.

Why? To answer that question, imagine this scene: A blind man and his dog are standing on a curb, waiting for a traffic light to change. When the light turns green, the dog is expected to escort the man across the street. However, a large car is speeding down the highway, not showing any signs of slowing down.

A dog that simply follows the rule, "Go on green lights," would lead his master into the path of a speeding car! However, a dog that is "intelligently disobedient" will disregard what his training has taught him. He will wait and see what the car is going to do. In other words, he breaks the rules!

How about you? Will you follow rules simply because that's the way you were taught? Or, will you evaluate your situation and make decisions based on your own ability to interpret the facts? Will you design your own destiny, or will you let outdated rules design it for you?

If you change your thinking, you CAN change your life—and your destiny!

10 RULES to BREAK

Rule Number 1

"Don't Waste Your Time with Dreams"

Those who lose dreaming are lost.
—Australian Aboriginal
proverb

Let's start this book with a TRUE story about a man who had a dream. Larry Walters had always wanted to fly. He joined the Air Force to become a pilot. Unfortunately, his eyesight was not good enough, and he left the service without ever learning how to fly.

Undaunted, he would sit in his lawn chair and watch commercial flights pass overhead. One day, he decided to join them. He went to the surplus store and purchased some large weather balloons. He filled them with helium and attached them to his lawn chair. He tied the lawn chair to his Jeep, and packed some sandwiches and drinks for what he imagined to be a short, leisurely flight above his neighborhood.

Now Larry was no dummy. He knew that he would eventually have to come down. So, he also packed along a pellet rifle. He planned to shoot out some of the balloons to gently lower himself to earth—AFTER he had realized his dream.

Unfortunately, the weather balloons provided more lift than Larry anticipated. In fact, he shot up to 11,000 feet before leveling off. The prevailing winds blew him into the air space for Los Angeles International Airport, where he was spotted by an incoming pilot. Imagine the surprise of the air traffic controllers when the pilot reported passing a man, in a lawn chair, with a rifle, at 11,000 feet!

Larry drifted for 14 hours, eventually being blown out to sea. He was finally rescued by a helicopter and brought back to land. When a reporter asked him why he did it, Larry replied, "Well, a man can't just sit around!"

There is a great lesson from this story. When you strive to achieve your dreams, your actions may seem silly to others. But remember, it is YOUR dream, not theirs. And if you have a dream, take Larry Walters' advice: DON'T JUST SIT AROUND—DO SOMETHING ABOUT IT!

Why We Should Have Dreams

The rule *Don't Waste Your Time with Dreams* is not only dumb, it is dangerous. (Well, perhaps not as dangerous as being in a lawn chair at 11,000 feet, but dangerous nonetheless.) You MUST dream. Without dreams, we are condemned to accept the status quo. Without dreams, we could never change anything.

Dreams motivate us and keep us going. When we face adversity, it is our dreams that hold us together. My wife, Jeanne, and I spend a great deal of time dreaming. We specifically list our dreams, when we will achieve them, and how they will change our lives.

Dreams are the essential forces in building wealth, strengthening relationships, or creating success. We can motivate other people if we know their dreams. Imagine the power of helping people get what they really want. They will be your friends for life.

Who Cares About Your Dreams?

Very few people have a solid dream. This leads to a multitude of problems. First, someone without a dream is unlikely to achieve happiness. Second, someone without a dream is certainly not likely to care about other people's dreams. So they're unlikely to ask anyone else the most important question in life, "What do you really want and how can I help you get it?"

It is amazing to me that people are so unconcerned about what other people want. Almost everyone needs to know what SOMEONE wants. How can you motivate another person if you have no idea what drives them?

In corporate America, we have certainly lost the knack of motivating others by helping them to really achieve their dreams. Perhaps it is different where you work. Does your boss ask you, "What is your greatest dream, and how can we help you achieve it?"

We cannot motivate ourselves to overcome the daily challenges of life unless we have a dream. We cannot motivate others unless we know what their dreams are. It is that simple.

Dreams And Reality

The rule to break for this chapter could easily have been called "Face Reality." Some younger people might say, "Get real." What they are all saying is, "Don't set your sights too high, you will be disappointed." You may feel that this is good advice. It protects people. But instead of protecting people, we should be showing them how to get what they want.

Most people shrink their dreams to fit into their perspective of reality. That is unfortunate—and wrong. We should be teaching ourselves and others to expand reality to reach our dreams!

Have you reduced your dreams? Have you begun to settle for compromise in life rather than demanding more? If you answered yes, you are certainly not alone. Most people are sitting in a comfort zone of their own creation. They have conveniently adjusted their dreams to fit into the reality of their lives. They have given up so much that they no longer even think about it.

How do we create a comfort zone? Let's take an example to illustrate the point. Consider a mythical couple in their thirties. Meet Jesse and Janice Johnson. They have been married for eight years and have two children, ages four and six. The Johnsons grew up in Detroit, but now they have a nice home in Florida.

Jesse is an engineer. Janice works for an insurance company as a claims adjustor. They have two incomes, two car payments, one mortgage, and little savings. In other words, they are typical.

Jesse drives a Chevrolet. He wanted a sports car, but it was too expensive and not really practical for his family. He likes to play golf, but the cost is very high. Besides, he works a lot and doesn't like to spend his weekends away from the family. Unfortunately, he ends up bringing work home on the weekends.

Janice doesn't like the idea of leaving her younger child in day care. Her older daughter goes to the day care after school until Janice can pick them up. Then, Janice rushes home to put dinner together.

Janice's parents have been sick this past year. Unfortunately, there hasn't been enough time or money to fly up to Detroit and visit them. Janice's sister lives there, so Janice assumes they are getting good care. She calls frequently, but only after five at night to save money.

The family vacations for two weeks per year. Usually, they drive to visit relatives. When they get back, Jesse works on all the things that he has put off doing—like painting the house and such. He doesn't really like spending vacation time on these chores.

Did this family have dreams when they were younger? They probably did. They imagined vacations, travel, nice cars, leisure time, and other "luxuries." They probably would like to have the money to take care of Janice's parents, take a "real vacation," and keep the kids at home rather than in day care. These are not just dreams. They are reasonable goals.

Do they have dreams now? Maybe they have small dreams now. Perhaps Jesse would like to develop his golf game. Perhaps Janice dreams of somehow enjoying her younger daughter's last year at home before school. But they probably avoid even thinking about it.

Why don't they have big dreams? Because if they had big dreams, as they did when they were younger, then the inability to reach those dreams would destroy them.

Why aren't they more concerned? Because they have surrounded themselves with other people who live the same way. They have reduced their expectations. Their friends, neighbors, and relatives are all in the same position.

You see, Jesse and Janice have rationalized their situation. They are willing to accept the way things are because they do not see a way to change it. Moreover, they are associating with other people who have also accepted the status quo.

By accepting, by being average, Jesse and Janice are in their comfort zone. Don't get me wrong. It is comfortable in the comfort zone. Once you accept the limitations of this zone, the anguish and frustration generally subside. Unfortunately, it is not really replaced with happiness or fulfillment, only acceptance.

What should they do? In my opinion, this couple needs to go a little wild! They need to seriously assess their situation and make some changes. But before they can take action, they need to do some serious dream building.

Jesse and Janice, like all of us, should ask, "What COULD life be like?" They need to VISUALIZE a different lifestyle. God did not create man to be average or mediocre. We are His greatest creation. This couple, like all of us, needs to live up to God's creative genius.

Jesse and Janice need to get a big, strong, overwhelming, and exciting dream. They need to ask some hard questions. They need to take a chance and attempt to fulfill their dreams.

Won't they be forced out of the comfort zone? Yes, but this is good. Sure it will cause them some discomfort. They will HUNGER for something. They will hunger for more. They will have to expand their reality to meet their new dreams. But if they can achieve their dreams, consider the lifestyle they could enjoy.

Why shouldn't Janice stay at home with the children—if she chooses to do so? Why shouldn't Jesse have two cars? Couldn't he have a sports car AND a family car? What would it be like for the couple to SHARE time with the children, enjoying the children's formative years? And what type of lessons would they then pass on to their kids? Should the lesson be to work hard, just to keep in the same mediocre place? Or, would the couple rather pass on a different lesson—identifying a worthwhile dream and then achieving it?

Dreams Can Make You Smile

Everyone has a different dream. Not everyone wants a car, a boat, or to stay at home with the kids. Some people do not want to travel. Some people do. Your dreams are a personal expression of your deepest desires. The real question is, "What do YOU want?"

The size and type of your dreams depend on what is happening in your life right now. I use the acronym S.M.I.L.E.S. to describe the stages of dreaming that most people move through. People's dreams will usually start out small and then grow with time and achievement.

Someone who is running out of money each month may not desire a large boat. On the other hand, a person who has attained all the material things he wants can begin to concentrate on a bigger dream. Let's look at S.M.I.L.E.S.

S — (Survival dreams.) These dreams are for people who have "more month than money." They may simply dream of the day when they can pay off their bills regularly. Making just enough to survive month to month is a fundamental problem for millions of people.

M — (Material dreams.) We are raised with the admonition that it is somehow bad to WANT things. On the contrary, it is all right to want material things. That is different than being materialistic. A materialistic person tries to own happiness by owning material goods.

Is there something you always dreamed of owning? How about that sports car, a nicer home, or a boat? Why not? There is nothing wrong with that!

I — (Income dreams.) Some people want income levels that are higher than they currently enjoy. My wife and I used to imagine how stable and free our lives would be if we could just reach a certain income level. The problem is that income usually depends on continued work. So, it is difficult to enjoy income unless you keep working.

Some smart individuals have found a way to generate RESIDUAL income. This is money that continues to come in even if you don't continue to work.

L — (Lifestyle dreams.) Why shouldn't you enjoy a great lifestyle? Lifestyle is a combination of money and the time to spend it. Many physicians have plenty of money, but because of the demands on their time, their lifestyles are the pits! Dream about the perfect lifestyle for you.

E — (Expressive dreams.) How would you live if you had everything you wanted: money, lifestyle, rewarding relationships, and so on. How would you express yourself? Some people play a musical instrument. Others learn foreign languages. Still others become more involved in the community and charity work.

Most people who have reached their expressive dream stage are already financially successful. Now, they can turn their pursuits to really interesting activities. They can grow personally, share with the community or family, and, in general, achieve their full human potential.

S — (Spiritual dreams.) Everyone has his own view of God and man's place on earth. It is my belief that the best way to serve God is to serve other people. This leads us to a greater understanding of the spiritual nature of life. We are expected to use our God-given talents to reach our full potential.

This is a dream of the highest order. Would you give money to your church, work in a mission, or assist family members? Once you have covered the other dreams, you have more freedom to pursue your spiritual dreams.

Of course, you don't have to be wealthy and retired to have a spiritual life. Even the poorest people can be deeply spiritual. But I'm talking about making a MAJOR impact on the well-being of others. This can take the form of either time or money. Unless you have taken care of these issues in your own life, however, it is very difficult to give freely to others.

Get A Dream

It is a fact that virtually no achievement, no matter how great or how small, would have been possible unless the individuals involved had a dream. Never forget that building a tree house for your kids and building the Great Wall of China both had the same humble beginnings—they started as dreams. Don't be held back by others. Do the research and get a dream!

Look Ahead

If you look ahead and see living the rest of your life as an "average person," you need a dream. Visualize yourself as a successful person who has achieved something worthwhile.

A Personal Note

My wife and I were introduced to the concept of dreaming a few years ago. We had become average people, mired in our comfort zone. Our dreams had shrunk to meet our reality.

True, we had a nice home, and my wife was a full-time mother. However, we had not clearly defined our real dreams. When we were shown how to visualize S.M.I.L.E.S., we got fired up. Now we are driven by truly exciting dreams.

We wrote and described our dreams on a large piece of poster board and tacked it up over our dresser. It is the first thing we see each morning and the last thing we read at night. We began to share our dreams, working together to make them come true.

Breaking the rule *Don't Waste Your Time with Dreams* has brought us closer together and has enabled us to move toward our destiny. Keep on dreaming!

10 RULES to BREAK

Rule Number 2

"The Best Things in Life Are Free"

The best things in life are NOT free—they are priceless!
—Bill Quain

It is a myth that the best things in life are free. Usually, this is a rationalization by people who do not have enough money or time to get what they really want. Get the facts. Don't fall into the trap of thinking you can have the best things without time and money. You cannot!

What Is Best In Life?

What do you consider to be the "best in life"? This is a highly personal topic. Here are some ideas that most of us would rank among the "best things in life."

Children: laughter, smiles, the first step, birth, recovery from illness, a hug, a kiss, "I love you," a present.

Nature:	the beach, the ocean, mountains, snowfall, blue skies, long summer days, a bird's song.
Family:	love, togetherness, holidays, security, commitment, heritage, caring.
People:	helping, friendship, companionship, excitement.
Spouse:	love, caring, sharing, planning, companionship, laughing, memories, growth.
Travel:	adventure, comfort, learning, fun, exercise.
Life:	growth, maturity, energy, youthfulness, wisdom, compassion.
Home:	security, comfort, beauty, nest.
Spirituality:	love, compassion, understanding, faith, freedom, belonging, promise.

Maybe you have some other things that you like. Whatever they are, they are not free. Priceless, maybe, but not free. Who can put a price on the smile of a child? What about your friendships, are they free? They are also priceless. There is no amount of money that can buy a true friend.

When we asked people to name the best things in life, very few mentioned material things. What would you think of a person who says that the best thing in life is a fast, expensive car? Is that the type of person you would trust? Of course not. Would you introduce your family to people who count ANY material possession as the best thing in life? Absolutely not.

Yet, we spend the majority of our lives pursuing material objects. We work at a job or a profession in order to pay bills. We miss the point. If we are constantly consumed with the accumulation of material things, we will not have time for the really beautiful things in life.

Beauty Is Fleeting

The laughter of your children is beautiful. The melodic sounds of a symphony playing one of the world's great compositions is beautiful. A sunset on a warm beach with a gentle breeze and a loved one to share it with is beautiful. Yet, all of these things are fleeting. It is this quality that makes them so rare. It is what makes them so beautiful.

Yes, the laughter can be recorded. So can the music. We can take a picture of the sunset. But none of these recordings will capture the thrill of the moment. Nothing will bring back the warm embrace of the person you love. The best things are very temporary. Miss them and they are gone forever.

Won't there be a sunset tomorrow? Yes, but it will belong to another day. Will the child not laugh again? Yes, but perhaps not in the same way. Won't our loved ones be here tomorrow? Perhaps not. Will you always be here tomorrow?

We assume that we can always recapture or recreate the moment. What arrogance we have. These moments are rare, agonizingly brief, and only to be lived as they happen. We chase the dream that SOMEDAY we will have the time to enjoy the best things in life. The problem is, by then they are gone.

Time And Temptation

Tonight, there is a beautiful sunset on a sandy beach. Will you be there? Or will you just be getting home from work, tired and irritable? Why aren't you there? Wouldn't you like to be?

So many people postpone the good things in life while they pursue a living. That is a shame. The good things are what make life beautiful. Yet, we are consumed by the need to make money. This is not a misplaced belief. We really do need money.

Some people go too far in the other direction. In my younger days, we used to call them "drop outs." They gave up their search for monetary rewards and went to live some place exotic. They stepped off of the fast track and decided to spend their time enjoying "the best things in life."

However, there is still a need for money and long-term security in life. We can choose to enjoy the good things now or postpone them till later. Either strategy has a price. If we enjoy them now, there may be no time to enjoy them later. With our incomes depleted, and our power to earn more money declining, the golden years may consist of tarnished brass for the drop outs.

Those who choose to make money now and enjoy the best things later face a very big gamble. Statistics show that most of us will never be able to stop working. Instead, we will always look ahead, never enjoying the moment. We will assume that, for some reason, things will get better. As we work away our lives, the best things go on without us—forever.

A Father's Story

There are those who have found a way to get the money-making portion of their lives out of the way and set up residual, willable income. These individuals work hard for a while. Then they use the income stream that they created to enjoy the best things in life. These people (and they are increasingly coming from the ranks of network marketers) use money to buy time. Time and money are all that is needed to enjoy the best things in life.

Let's look at two individuals. The first is a fictitious character named Bob. The second is an actual person named Bruce. Bruce's story is absolutely true, word for word. Bob's story is the story of most men. One broke the rules, the other followed them. Which one has the best things in life?

Bob

It doesn't matter how old Bob is. He could be in his twenties, thirties, or forties. He has a job. He is honest and good-natured and loves his family.

After work one day, he picks up his two children from the full-time baby sitter. Bob and his wife are happy that the kids can go to a private home rather than a day care center. In fact, Bob works extra projects each year to make the money necessary to place the kids in this care.

"Guess what?" bubbles the baby sitter. "Bob Junior took his first step today." "That's fantastic!" Bob says. "Maybe he'll take another one at home tonight." Bob rushes home and tells his wife. She is getting in from work a little late. They quickly feed the baby, give him a bath, and then go to the playroom to take some pictures.

Indeed, little Robert does take another step. The proud parents take many snapshots and video footage. Yet, the first step had already been taken. The pictures merely recorded the first step that the baby made IN THE PRESENCE OF HIS PARENTS! It will be that way for the rest of their lives.

Bruce (A True Story)

Bruce is a retired coach who has developed a thriving business in network marketing. Recently, he asked his ten-year-old daughter, a straight "A" student, if she had anything important in school the next day. When she said no, Bruce told her of his plan.

He had made reservations for breakfast at a private business club. He took his daughter there for a leisurely morning. Everyone else in the club was having a "power breakfast" with business clients. What a contrast they must have made!

Bruce knew his daughter loved Barbie dolls, so he had purchased five dolls and wrapped them. The waiters delivered them during the meal. After breakfast, this retired coach spent the morning with his daughter, playing dolls. Why did he play dolls? Because that is what she wanted. It was a wonderful experience for both of them. Was it free? No. It was priceless.

Mothers, fathers, sons, daughters, singles, couples: We all should have the opportunities to enjoy the best things in life. In order to do so, however, we must make some hard choices. We must make decisions that determine our futures AND our families' futures.

Get Free

The whole concept of this book is about designing your destiny. I am not urging you to simply make a lot of money. I am telling you that you have the capability to become free. There are systems for creating residual income that will free your time and create financial security. You will then have choices in life that allow you to enjoy the best things.

Are you able to relax and enjoy your life? Or are you like most people today, worried about the future, stressed out from a lack of time and money? You need time. You need peace of mind. You need security.

If you do not learn to break the rules, then you will live as a virtual slave. Worse, you might condemn future generations of your family to do the same. It's never too late. No matter how old you are, you can make the decision today that will change your life.

How much have you already missed? Have you been truly enjoying life, or have you just been struggling to make a go of it? Make yesterday the last day you spend on earth without the best things in life. Start today, right now, with a plan to recapture your soul!

A Personal Note

In the Quain household, we believe in vacations! They are important to us, so we take a lot of them. We are able to do
(continued on next page)

this because we made some hard choices earlier in our lives—choices to break free of the "rules" that govern the average person's life. Now, we are reaping the rewards.

Each year, we have a family reunion in Ocean City, New Jersey. My parents, brother, and sisters from six different locations all rent houses in this great old seashore resort. My wife, Jeanne, and I bring our kids so that they can get to know their cousins. It is a great time.

This family time is one of the best things in life to me. It won't last forever. Already, the older cousins have sports, camp, and other activities that make it more difficult to get together. Parents grow older, kids have other interests. Yet, each year we have somehow made the time for this two-week event.

For my wife and me, the vacation is relaxing. This year, I turned down some speaking engagements so that we could have uninterrupted time. The money I would have made cannot compare to the time spent with our family and our lifelong friends.

We take other vacations each year, traveling to exciting, beautiful spots. Without the time to take the other vacations, I don't believe the family-oriented weeks at the "shore" would be quite as enjoyable. We are not thinking, "Maybe we should have gone someplace else this year on our two weeks off."

We have discovered that the best things in life take *time and money* to enjoy.

Rule Number 3

"You're Too Young to Retire"

No one ever said on his death bed,
"Gee, if I'd only spent more time at the office."
—H. Jackson Brown, Jr.

Because of my poor eyesight, I need partners with great eyes to spot the ball for me when I play golf. That's why I love the story about an old man who had recently retired and loved to play the game.

The old man had a friend who, like me, was visually impaired. "Can you see well?" the almost-blind man asked the old fellow. "Like a hawk," said the old man. So, the two played together. The visually impaired man hit a terrific drive on the first tee. "Did you see where it went?" he asked the old man. "Oh, yes," said the old fellow. "Where did it go?" asked the visually impaired friend. "I forget," replied the old man.

The moral of the story: Why not retire early and enjoy life while you can, instead of waiting until you are too infirm to really enjoy it? Don't wait until you are given the time. MAKE the time NOW!

What are your plans for retirement? Do you picture yourself in your sixties, playing golf and going to the early bird special at the local restaurant? Or do you envision a youthful, vigorous retirement, packed with adventures, learning, and enjoyment?

For most people, retirement is an age, not a state of mind. Most people plan on working well into their later years. The official retirement age in the United States is 65. However, many people will be unable to retire at this point. *Money* magazine says that people will face many obstacles at retirement age, including the fact that many will have to continue working.

Wait a second. Look at that again. If you must keep working, how do you know that you are retired? In fact, that is a contradiction in terms, like the term "jumbo shrimp." When I retire, I don't want to work at a job!

Two Problems

There are two major assumptions that most people make when they think of retirement. First, they assume that they will retire at the end of their life. Second, they assume that they will have the money to do the things they want. The first one is self-imposed, the second is self-deluding.

Retiring at the end of a long career is self-imposed. Why should we have to wait until our late sixties to stop working 40 to 50 hours per week? The reason is simple. Most people simply ASSUME that they will have to do it. It is not hard to imagine why they think this is the way it should be. In all of their experience, most people never know anyone who has retired early.

We have read stories of some genius millionaire who invented a new widget or gadget and is living off the proceeds. We know they are out there, but does anyone actually KNOW one of these whiz kids? Would you let your daughter marry one?

The truth is that we are programmed to believe that retirement is out of reach until we are too old to really enjoy it. That's a shame, because most people end up postponing some of the finest experiences in life, waiting for retirement.

We go to work in our late teens or early twenties and we continue working until we are in our late sixties. Few ever question it—most never even think about it. Look at any train station or bus stop on a Monday morning. Everyone is lined up, ready to start another week. The freeways are jammed with commuters.

"But wait," you say. "These people find great rewards from their work. It helps to define who they are. If they retired, what would they do all day? They would be bored, unhappy, and lost, wouldn't they?"

Before considering how boring it might be to retire early, let's go to the second point in this discussion. What would possibly make anyone think that if he were living month to month for fifty years, he suddenly would have money to spend at retirement?

In his book, *The Seven Laws Of Money*, Michael Phillips makes an interesting observation about this very point. The author says that people have delusions about money. For example, most people imagine that they could do a lot more in their lives if they only had more money. They imagine retirement as "free time." They picture themselves without monetary concerns. But for most people, retirement is riddled with concerns about money, and there is no income from a job!

Many financial experts warn us that people will need to continue working after they retire. They will not do this to feel fulfilled. Working as a proud senior citizen at a fast food restaurant is not especially rewarding or loaded with esteem—despite the commercials.

In fact, many people delude themselves with the expectation that when they finally stop working, they will magically have time and money. This image is so compelling that they really do postpone the important things—time with family, celebrations, trips, leisure pursuits—hoping for the day to come when, suddenly, they will stop working and have time and money.

The Problem With Postponement

The old saying "Time and tide wait for no man" is true, no matter how much we wish it otherwise. A child's birthday can never be repeated. Your parents' anniversary, your spouse's need for companionship during a decision or crisis, all of these things are fleeting. Missing them means missing life. Will they wait for your retirement?

In the end, will you regret the things you missed by working? And finally, as you look back on life, will you say, "I wish I had worked one more day?"

According to *The Inventurers: Excursions In Life And Career Renewal*, postponing the rewards of life is much too common. The authors cite insurance industry studies to point out the dangers inherent in waiting for our "just rewards." Only about 10 percent of the people born in the United States will live until retirement AND have financial independence. For the remaining 90 percent:

> **36% die before 65**
> **54% are broke at retirement**
> **90% are dead or dead broke!**

The Nature Of Retirement

Because we are so programmed to consider retirement as the lifestyle of senior citizens, we find it difficult to imagine that it will be fulfilling for younger people. We also assume that there is no way to accumulate enough money in our younger lives to retire on. Both of these misconceptions can prevent us from really enjoying the fruits of a free enterprise system.

It is only because we have the advantages of free enterprise that we can even consider an alternative to the life-long sentence imposed by most people on themselves. Free enterprise allows us to create financial security.

Under a free enterprise system, income does not have to stop when you retire. Did that get your attention? Did you envision living off your investments, Social Security, pensions, and the kindness of your relatives when you retired? If you did, it is probably because you have not yet learned how to break the rules.

That's why I encourage people to get involved in a system that allows them to build a business that will continue to provide income, whether they work or not. It's called *residual income*. There are systems and teachers who can show you how to do it.

Now, what if you had money AND the time to enjoy it? Would that change your mind about retirement? And, what if you had a growing, thriving business that did not require your daily attention? Suppose that this business got bigger each day, bringing in more money to you and your family. Instead of worrying about outliving your money, you would only worry about how you were going to spend it!

Would you find fulfilling, rewarding things to do with your life and your money? Of course you would. If you had time AND money, you would find a way to keep from being bored.

So, retirement is not what you think. Perhaps you will want to partially retire at an early age. You can work for a while and then take a vacation. I have met some free enterprise participants lately who are on the "vacation of the month" club. Why not?

A Personal Note

I want to retire early. Why not? I am not afraid of being
idle or bored. I AM afraid of being lonely, because I know
that many of my friends will not be able to retire early.
That is why I associate with people who have the same
early retirement dream as mine—people who will break
this rule and design their own destiny.

There are so many things I want to do in life. But, taking
extended vacations, traveling, and having personal and
family adventures are difficult to do if I must report to
another person on a JOB. And the things I REALLY like
to do, like boating, biking, and skiing, are more fun when
you're younger. I don't want to wait for my "golden
years" to have great fun. I'd like to do it NOW!

10 RULES to BREAK

Rule Number 4

"Don't Rock the Boat"

New opinions are always suspected,
and usually opposed, without any other reason
but because they are not already common.
                                              —J. Locke

Here is a personal example of how it can be difficult for anyone to "rock the boat." Recently, Steve Lebruto, a CPA and educator, came to me with an idea. He said most people would not have enough money to retire. He suggested that they were being misled by financial advisors who assured them that, through stocks, funds, or retirement accounts, they would have a wealthy retirement. We ran the numbers and found out some startling facts. The results are published in a pamphlet called *Your Personal Financial Calculator* (PFC).

The PFC certainly paints a different picture than conventional wisdom. Using the PFC, readers can calculate their financial status by themselves. They actually choose their own predicted inflation and interest rate. Using a table and easy charts, they can then determine:

What their current salaries or incomes will be worth when they retire.

How much money they need in their retirement accounts.

How much money they will need to save, EACH AND EVERY YEAR, in order to have that retirement account.

We were astonished at the results. For example, a thirty-year-old couple, with a combined income of $60,000 per year, will need more than $2.3 MILLION in their retirement account, assuming a 4 percent inflation rate and a 7 percent annual return on investments, in order to continue to live at their current level after they retire. In order to achieve this, they will need to save MORE THAN $24,000 EACH YEAR, beginning RIGHT NOW! If they miss a year, they will have to increase the amount substantially in order to catch up.

(By the way, in order to have the same purchasing power that a $60,000 income brings today, you will need $194,000 per year 35 years from now.)

Does this sound like what financial planners are telling people? It didn't sound like it to us. All we heard were sales pitches for mutual funds. Even planners who were independent and did not have a particular fund to sell were not telling us it would be almost impossible to achieve our goals.

So, what was our first thought? Did we immediately call the newspapers and spread the word? No. Even though Steve has CPA credentials and I have conducted extensive research on personal finances, we were uncertain. Our first thought was "How could we have discovered this? Why didn't the others see this?"

This creeping uncertainty overtakes almost everyone when they start to rock the boat. It is inevitable. We are trained to accept certain facts, certain rules. That is why I wrote this book. I WANT to rock your boat. It needs to be rocked.

Break This Rule!

"Don't rock the boat" could be written several ways. I could also say, "We have always done things that way." In any case, this sentiment is dangerous, and could cost you a fortune.

Someone who rocks the boat is considered a trouble maker. Yet, it is often those people who have the creativity, drive, and initiative to challenge the status quo.

Copernicus and Galileo rocked the boat. Edison and Ford are counted among this number. Ronald Reagan did things that only an eccentric would have tried—and the Berlin Wall came tumbling down. Carry Nation and other leaders of the suffragette movement in the United States CERTAINLY rocked the boat. Thanks to them, women have the right to vote.

What about you? Have you been warned against making waves? What do you do to challenge the way things have always been done? Do you simply accept the fact that you are too small or unimportant to chart a new course?

How A Different Way Is Better

I talk to many people who dared to view the world differently. Almost all of them describe a feeling of disbelief—not in others, but in themselves. They simply cannot believe that THEY could have made a discovery that escaped most people.

It takes tremendous courage to challenge the current beliefs. It takes even greater courage to act upon your convictions in a positive manner. That is what makes the rule *Don't Rock the Boat* so hard to break. We are afraid of being wrong, of making assumptions that we feel we are not QUALIFIED to make.

Understanding Versus Action

Even among those few people who do see the same foolishness you recognize, even fewer will take action. You see, there is a HUGE difference between people who recognize something and those who actually take action. Taking action is a lost art in today's society.

Saying "I couldn't possibly see something that all those experts missed" is an excuse. Sure, it is safe, and it does prevent us from sticking out our necks. We will find peace in the very act of being "average." Of course, the average person is doomed to mediocrity.

The above-average person takes action. Your actions should be carefully planned and executed. They are the positive steps toward becoming above average—and having the things above-average people enjoy—such as above-average houses, incomes, lifestyles, and the like.

When They Say, "Calm Down," SCREAM!

Many people will tell you to calm down. They are a little put off if you start getting passionate or excited about a subject. It worries them. They might change the subject, stop answering your phone calls, avoid you. They don't want to be around someone who is rocking the boat. So they ask you, or tell you, to calm down.

NEVER, NEVER, NEVER calm down. Get excited and stay excited. Put energy into your whole being and fill yourself with hope and unabashed emotion. Go for it!

Unabashed emotion, of course, doesn't mean you have to be a jerk. Read and follow the advice found in *How To Win Friends And Influence People* by Dale Carnegie. Your ideas are worth sharing. You should help others to understand what you do. You want to encourage the people you love to take positive action. This can only be done by learning how to get along with people.

On the other hand, you will never get anyone else charged up about your ideas if you calm down. Get excited, become a whirlwind, and use the momentum to take positive action to achieve worthwhile goals.

When They Say, "We've Always Done It That Way," SCREAM!

This excuse is used by anyone who doesn't want to experience change. Today, some things MUST be done differently! In this time of rapidly changing technology, procedures are out of date within a matter of months in many cases. Would you refuse to get money from your ATM machine because that is not the way your parents did it? When I was young, no one would even THINK about pumping their own gas at a service station. Today, everybody pulls into self-service gas stations.

Refusing to change because things have always been done a certain way is lazy. It ignores the responsibility of the individual to adapt, improvise, and overcome.

Don't Rock the Boat? Break this rule! Don't be trapped by the past. If you are, then you cannot have any more success in the future than you have had in the past.

A Personal Note

There is a restaurant on the west coast of Florida called Yellowtail. On the bottom of the menu it says, "We'll do anything you want, just give us a buck." What a great idea!

I ordered a tuna steak sandwich that came with homemade potato chips. I gave the waiter $1 to substitute coleslaw.

(continued on next page)

"Fine," he said, "but our homemade chips are fantastic. They are spiced with jalapeno peppers and cooked to order." "Great," I said. "Here's another dollar, change it back to the chips!" He let me rock the boat. I was willing to pay for it!

Pay the price and design your own destiny. Don't be afraid to be different—*be afraid to be average!*

Rule Number 5

"Build a Better Mousetrap and the World Will Beat a Path to Your Door"

Don't sell the steak; sell the sizzle.
It is the sizzle that sells the steak and not the cow,
although the cow is, of course, mighty important.
—Elmer Wheeler

There is a story about a man driving 50 miles per hour down a country road. He suddenly notices a chicken running beside him. The man speeds up to 60 miles per hour; the chicken speeds up. The man speeds up to 70 miles per hour; the chicken speeds up. The man takes a close look at the chicken. It has three legs! The chicken pulls ahead of the man and turns down a dirt road. The man decides to follow and discover more about this remarkable chicken.

He comes to a barn, and a farmer is standing outside. "Did you see that?" cries the man. "What, the three-legged chicken?" asks the farmer. "We raise them here. You see, I like a drumstick, my wife likes a drumstick, and my son likes a drumstick. This way we each get one." "That's amazing," says the man. "How do they taste?" "Don't know," says the farmer. "Never could catch one!"

This story is funny, for sure, but it points out a serious lesson in business. Just because a product is better doesn't mean it will automatically be in demand. Fact is, products don't sell themselves. People sell the products.

The "better mousetrap" rule says that a great product will sell itself. Supposedly, there are people out there who are searching for better products, and they will find YOU if you have developed one.

The truth is, a new or innovative product, no matter how remarkable it is, is not a guarantee that the world will notice or care. Conversely (and this is the REAL IMPORTANT POINT HERE), it is not always the best product that is the most successful.

Products That Never Made It

According to *Newsweek* magazine, the U.S. Patent Office has issued more than two million patents since 1971. In order to get a patent, the new product must be completely different from other patented items. Patent applications undergo intense scrutiny. In most cases, the inventor must build a working model, or at least have professional drawings and specifications.

Despite this intense scrutiny and preparation, most patents never become commercially produced. Even if they are manufactured, the demand for them is often so small that the investment is never recouped. These "better mousetraps" sit on the shelf and are forgotten.

There are many examples. For this book, we will examine three products and their struggle for success.

Another Man And His Chicken

Colonel Sanders was a small restaurant operator. He had discovered a better way to cook chicken. He combined pressurized frying with 21 secret herbs and spices to create a unique product. People loved his chicken. His recipe was the toast of his small town.

Even more importantly, the method of cooking was fast. He was able to reduce costs and create a high volume. These two factors would naturally appeal to restaurateurs who were eager for fast, economical, customer-pleasing new foods. Right? Nope!

Did restaurant owners visit his stores, begging for the secret of cheap chicken? Did giant food companies telephone him, asking for permission to purchase and resell the prized poultry? Did customers arrive from other states, ready to stand in long lines, to do whatever it took to have a mouthful of his fabulous fowl?

The answer, of course, is no. No one was really interested in the chicken. The restaurant industry did not see its potential. The food giants did not comprehend the possibilities. Consumers had no idea the stuff was so tasty. It took many years of hard work for Colonel Harland Sanders to crisscross the country, showing individual restaurant operators the results of his innovative techniques.

(In fact, Colonel Sanders went broke because a new highway was built that by-passed his original restaurant. People were not even willing to drive a few extra miles to get this great product.)

Not only have I read about the relentless pursuit that the Colonel undertook, I have also met people who were shown the process. A man in New York state who owned a small restaurant told me of his encounter with the Colonel. He said that a strange-looking man came to the back door of the restaurant one day. The man, Colonel Sanders, had a station wagon filled with equipment. The Colonel showed my friend the secret of making fried chicken quickly and then offered to sell him a franchise.

My friend laughed at Colonel Sanders. He couldn't imagine that it would be worthwhile to pay this guy for a chicken recipe, let alone a franchise. When I met my friend, he was a professor in a small community college. Imagine how his life would have been different if he had only listened to the Colonel. How many other people refused the opportunity? It just goes to show you that a good product is not enough!

Plug Me In

Gasoline-powered cars are the major source of air pollution for most cities. What is a possible cure? Trade in our gas guzzlers for an electric car? Electric cars have been available for some time. Sure, they are slower and less convenient. Yet, they are non-polluting, quiet, inexpensive to run, and ample for many forms of commuting or errand-running. They hold the promise to free us from dependency on foreign oil.

The technology may be a bit primitive, and many people don't want to give up their fast cars with lots of room. That's not the point. This electric car is, in many respects, a better mousetrap. Is the world beating a path to this door?

It will take a lot more than a good product to convince people that they should switch to an electric car. Municipalities will be hesitant to embrace the new technology, despite its promise. Certainly, car dealers are not going to jeopardize their franchises by selling electric cars. They don't know HOW to do it, and they just don't WANT to do it.

The Care Chair

My mother, Kay Quain, is an inventor, author, and publisher. About 15 years ago, she was diagnosed with cancer. She spent many weeks in the hospital while undergoing operations and chemotherapy. During this ordeal, she was often confined to a hospital bed. Her friends and family visited her regularly.

While lying in bed, she noticed that there were no seats available for visitors, other than the low chairs at the foot of the bed. She, like all patients, was not able to see her visitors when they sat in these chairs. The chairs were too heavy to easily pull around to the side of the bed. Even after moving them, they were still too low, and were in the way of the nurses and doctors.

The doctors didn't have any place to sit either. The nurses, technicians, and other hospital personnel were similarly without a comfortable seat. Perhaps, my mother thought, this is one of the reasons that the doctors and nurses spend so little time with the patients. There was no way to sit and be eye to eye with the critically ill, frightened, and lonely patient. Was this any way to cure medical problems?

When she was cured of her cancer, after three years of weekly chemotherapy treatments, my mother went to work on an invention. She created an aluminum chair that put the visitor and health professional at the correct height to talk with the patient. The chair was quickly foldable so it could be moved in case of an emergency. It was safe and easy to clean. Best of all, she applied for, and received, a U.S. patent for "The Care Chair."

Is this invention available in any hospitals? No. Is there a demand for it? Absolutely. Several hospitals saw the prototype and immediately wanted to place orders. Then what is the problem? Manufacturers are reluctant to introduce new products into the medical field. The cost of obtaining approval from government regulators is staggering. In addition, the liability insurance is outrageously expensive. The result? This better mousetrap is patented, but not available. The world did not beat a path to her door!

A Better Burger?

On the other hand, there is McDonald's. This hamburger chain has been extremely successful by anyone's standards. Is it because they have a better product? Well, opinions may vary, but for most of us, the food is not superior to a really good hamburger that we can make at home.

In the 1960s, when the McDonald's system was first introduced, their fast, small, and bland hamburgers were not the best in town. Certainly, their milkshakes are not as good as the "old-fashioned" kind. Yet, because of their command of the distribution process, this chain has revolutionized the way we eat.

Colonel Sanders eventually made it big, too. Why did it take him so long? He spent too many years focusing on the PRODUCT rather than the DELIVERY SYSTEM. When he finally did make it big, it wasn't because people beat a path to his door. It was because he found a way to beat a path to theirs!

There are many success stories in which the products, although acceptable, are not the best available. Yet, because their organizations found some way to go out and put the products into consumers' hands, the money rolled in.

Distribution And Incentives—The Keys To Mousetrap Sales

Rich DeVos and Jay Van Andel figured it out. These two pioneers of modern free enterprise combined excellent products with the means of getting them into the hands of consumers. They founded the Amway Corporation and revolutionized modern business practices throughout the world.

They had wonderful products. Their soaps were not only effective, they were biodegradable. The packaging was minimized to reduce waste. In fact, the company has won numerous awards for its environment-friendly practices.

But, good products weren't enough. If the Amway organization simply depended on good products, it would not have recorded billions and billions in sales every year. The marvelous products would have stayed right in Michigan, where Amway is headquartered. Households in countries from North America to Australia, and all stops in between, would not be using the Amway goods and services if they were simply great products!

What DeVos and Van Andel figured out was that it took DISTRIBUTION to move products. Equally as important, people must have some INCENTIVE to help move those products through the distribution channels.

DeVos and Van Andel have built an organization that is unequaled in terms of loyalty and efficiency. It is efficient because goods and services move quickly, and at low cost, to the consumers. It is motivating because the distributors make money by doing it.

This simple system is so powerful that today almost 90 percent of the Fortune 500 companies have partnered with Amway. These prestigious and renowned organizations use the distribution/incentive system to place their goods in the hands of motivated consumers.

A Personal Note

I teach in the College of Business at the University of Central Florida in Orlando. The business department there teaches traditional courses in accounting, cost control, management, and the like—all very important and essential for business success. What we don't teach, however, is how to motivate people and how to make money. And what we don't teach is that there are some rules that need to be broken.

(continued on next page)

Learn to identify the real keys to creating wealth. It's not about building a better mousetrap! It's about finding out what people want, finding it for them, and putting it into their hands. In order to do this successfully, motivate people by providing meaningful, unlimited rewards.

Rule Number 6

"You Can't Be in Two Places at the Same Time"

Remember that time is money.
—Benjamin Franklin

You Can't Be in Two Places at the Same Time. Here is an indisputable law of physics. If something is here, then how can it be over there?

Perhaps I am speaking in a metaphor. Do I mean that you can't PHYSICALLY be in two places, but you can MENTALLY be in two places? No. I mean you CAN literally be in two places at one time.

In fact, if you want to be successful today, you MUST create a system that puts you in at least two places at the same time. I suggest you should look for a system that puts you in THOUSANDS of places at the same time.

How To Break This Rule

There are two major ways to break the rule *You Can't Be in Two Places at the Same Time.* First, use technology to live and work in two places at the same time. Second, use some form of a network system to accomplish the same thing.

Technology

Technology has fundamentally altered our ability to work, play, and communicate—any time and anywhere. Computers, fax machines, E-mail, cellular phones, and digital pagers are relatively inexpensive and not difficult to master. Yet, technology's "artificial brains," like the human brain, are not used to their full potential. Here is a simple test to prove this point.

Visit 10 people in their homes. How many of them have a VCR that flashes "12:00 a.m.," even if you're visiting in the middle of the afternoon? Why? Because most people with VCRs haven't figured out how to set the automatic clock. The VCR is a simple gadget; almost every home in America has at least one. Yet, most of us are not able to use the VCR to its full potential.

Our house is no exception. My wife has figured out how to set the time on the VCR. However, we still haven't figured out how to record shows on a channel other than the one we are watching.

On the other hand, Jeanne and I have cellular phones, voice mail, a desktop fax, and other machines, that allow us to utilize our time more efficiently. We can go on vacation, leave the computer on, retrieve messages, and get work done while in transit. I have a portable computer that is useful for all sorts of tasks.

So, we are improving.

The point is, with all the technology at our disposal, we are now able to be in two places at once. If you want proof, look to EPCOT Center at Disney World.

A few short years ago, their futuristic exhibits featured, among other things, a woman sitting at a computer in her house. She was shopping while watching her children and probably cooking dinner. What a marvel!

However, the exhibit was removed. Why? Because this is no longer futuristic. It is here. As George Allen used to say, "The future is now!"

Many companies are now allowing their employees to work from home by using telecommunication. It reduces commuting time, allows for greater flexibility, improves morale, and, most importantly, puts them in two places at once.

Networking—Duplication Made Easy

Have you ever thought, "I wish there were two of me"? Parents are especially prone to uttering this statement. When you are being pulled in so many directions at once that you are afraid you will snap, it's time to break the rules.

Since the Industrial Revolution, we have traded time for money. That is, we work for someone who gives us money. If we don't work, we don't get paid. Most people accept this rule as a fact. It doesn't have to be this way.

Today, we live in a NETWORK society. Networks are teams of people who work together to achieve a common goal. However, networks differ greatly from other organizations. In a typical corporation, for example, people work together for the good of the organization. In a network, participants have personal goals that can be achieved faster or better by utilizing the talents of everyone in the system. The trick is to make sure that EVERYONE gets something out of the network.

Many well-known business consultants and writers are now extolling the merits of a network. John Naisbait, the author of *Megatrends 2000*, predicted the rise of the network. Peter Drucker, perhaps the father of modern management principles for the 21st century, explains the use of networks in his article "The Network Society" (*Tempdigest,* Winter, 1996).

According to Drucker, layoffs and downsizing have fundamentally changed the way we view our loyalty to the organization. In the 1950s, societies throughout the world began to develop the "Organization Man." This individual worked for a corporation or other large organization. The organization took care of him, gave him security, and accepted loyalty. That has certainly changed.

Drucker asserts that these people still work *at* the organization, but not *for* the organization. In other words, they have been laid off and are now outsourced workers. They may do the same job, yet they are not part of the permanent work force. They use networks to find temporary jobs. They contribute to corporate goals, but they are always mindful of their own needs.

Actually, this is not always bad. Many people are happier working for themselves. They enjoy the freedom. And, with technology and networking, they are able to be in two places at once.

My friend Dennis worked for a large corporation in Florida. A few years ago, he and a partner began to develop a computer program that would make his job easier. His partner was self-employed, and the duo worked on the project on their own time, using their own equipment at Dennis' house.

One day, Dennis' boss found out about the project from another company. He called Dennis into his office and told him to either give up his private venture or resign. Dennis had three days to make up his mind.

When Dennis met his boss on the deadline day, he said he would resign. The boss said he hadn't expected that response, so he told Dennis to forget the whole conversation and keep working for the company. But Dennis had already made up his mind. The result—Dennis now works three days per week for the company as a consultant. He makes twice his old salary and is doing quite nicely with the computer program as well.

Dennis is now part of a network of professionals who use their skills to serve themselves and an organization. He is now "Network Man," not "Organization Man."

Duplicate, Duplicate

Networking is only the start, however. To truly be in two places at once, it is necessary to duplicate yourself. This is the real key to being in two places at once. If you are duplicated, your partner or team member can do the very same thing you would have done if you were actually there.

Some people, especially highly skilled professionals, cannot be duplicated. A surgeon cannot find a replacement in the phone book. However, teams of physicians, working together, can duplicate each other.

There is an old story about duplication. A two-acre pond had a lily pad colony. Each day, the population of lily pads doubled. It started out with one lily pad. On the second day, there were two pads, on the third day, four, and so on. It wasn't long before half the pond—one acre—was completely covered.

Two fishermen sat in their boat in the middle of that pond. The pond was now half covered with lily pads. The first one said, "There are sure a lot of lily pads out here." "Well," said the second, "half the lake is still open. We still have a full acre left for fishing. We can fish the rest of the week without any problems."

The next day, the number of lily pads again doubled, and the pond was completely covered.

This is the power of duplication. Through duplication, a task that seems impossible can be accomplished.

Network marketing companies have made duplication an art form. They have simplified their systems to make EVERYTHING duplicatable. In fact, if it can't be easily duplicated, these companies will usually not attempt it.

Duplication can only work when there is a well-defined system that can be performed by almost anyone. People who practice duplication put their egos on hold. They realize that there is no profit in being a star. A star must be present for the performance. A duplicated person can be anywhere.

Consider the case of a major star in a Broadway play. Sure, there is an understudy. But, imagine how disappointed the audience will be if they pay an exorbitant ticket price, only to find that the star of the show has taken a day off. Even if the understudy knows all the lines by heart, is a great dancer, and can sing like Pavarotti, it is not the same. A star can not be in two places at the same time.

However, a networker can be. Consultants, physician teams, network marketers—anyone who can be duplicated can be in two places, doing the same thing, drawing the same benefits. In fact, the benefits are also duplicated.

You CAN be in two places at the same time!

A Personal Note

As I mentioned several times in this book, I am legally blind. I cannot drive a car, read printed material, and such.

However, technology allows me to overcome many of the obstacles I face. My fax machine makes it easy to deliver

(continued on next page)

documents across town, so I don't have to drive. My computer links me to anyone in the world. My computer is equipped with a "screen reader" that actually uses a human voice to read the screen to me. I am also able to shop from home, at all hours. In other words, I'm able to be in more than one place at a time, even with my disability! If I can break this rule, surely you can!

Because I have put myself in more than one place at any time, my wealth has increased. This year I bought a car and hired drivers to increase my freedom. That's why I encourage people to use technology and duplicate their time by networking. It works!

10 RULES to BREAK

Rule Number 7

"Hard Work Is Its Own Reward"

Sudden realization:
The pay's the same no matter what I do.
—Dilbert,
by Scott Adams

Have you heard the story about the guy named Horace? He read an ad in the newspaper that said, "Enjoy a free, two-week cruise in the Caribbean. Just show up on Pier 52 in Miami on October 21." Horace reported to the pier, and announced he was there for the free two-week cruise. Suddenly, two huge men threw a bag over his head and knocked him unconscious. Horace awoke several hours later with a terrible drumming in his head.

To his horror, he realized he was chained to a giant oar, and the drumming came from the front of the ship. "Boom, boom, boom," went the drum. "Row, row, row," shouted the drummer. For two weeks, Horace and his unfortunate companions rowed the ship around the Caribbean.

When he was freed, Horace stood on the dock, rubbing his sore wrists. He noticed the man who had been chained next to him. Horace said, "I have a question. Are we supposed to tip the drummer?" "Well," replied his companion, "it's up to you, but we tipped him last year."

The moral of this story is: It's bad enough that people expect us to do hard work with no apparent rewards. But it's even worse that many of us eagerly participate in this system!

How many people do you know who earn 10 dollars an hour in a job they hate, only to get laid off? So what do they do? They apply for the same job with another company so they can earn (you got it!) 10 dollars an hour at a job they hate. That's like tipping the drummer!

Have you ever heard the following words at work: "We need to work hard and put in some extra effort to create something we can all be proud of. Unfortunately the budget is really tight this year, so we can't expect any more money. But, we will have a great sense of accomplishment."

OR

"If you wanted to get rich, you shouldn't have gotten into this line of work."

OR

"We're all part of a team here. Let's work together for the good of the organization."

If you have ever heard these statements, or even worse, if you have used them yourself, this chapter, *Hard Work Is Its Own Reward*, is dedicated to you.

Why Should You Expect A Reward?

In the "Rules to Make" section of this book, we will further discuss the need for rewards. For now, let's just say this: Anytime you do something, you have a right to expect some benefit from it. The reward does not have to be in the form of money. It can be a simple thank you. However, all people need some reward, some show of appreciation for their work.

Remember, you were not created to spend a life in hard toil, providing rewards for someone else.

Have you ever noticed how hard some people have to work just to get minimum wage? Picture ditch diggers or roofers, working in the hot summer sun. Do you think they'd say hard work is its own reward? Not on your life!

The Two-edged Sword

Like so many things, there are two sides to consider. First, let's accept the fact that hard work is not its own reward. Second, let's agree that rewards do motivate you. We must also conclude that rewards will motivate others.

When an executive attempts to motivate people by appealing to their sense of loyalty to the corporation or organization, he or she is almost always in line for some reward if the work is completed. This fact is not lost on the worker!

The fact is, if you want to motivate someone else, you must reward them. Don't expect others to do what you will not. And don't be fooled by someone who complies with your command without a corresponding incentive. They may appear to be excited about the prospect of performing more work for the good of the organization. However, they may plan their revenge through some form of sabotage.

Dale Carnegie stresses this point in the very first chapter of his blockbuster book *How To Win Friends And Influence People*. Richard Huseman, Ph.D., also proposes the same sentiments in *Managing The Equity Factor*. In fact, Huseman believes that people will seek a balance between their input and the output they experience at work.

In Shakespeare's *Hamlet,* we hear the phrase "Neither a borrower nor a lender be." The principles of this statement apply here. We might paraphrase it as "Neither a slave nor a slave owner be." Don't work simply for the sake of working. Don't ask others to do it, either.

Don't Make The Trade

Some people rationalize the situation by assuming that they are trading a bit of pride for financial security. They work hard, doing things they don't want to do, just to keep their jobs.

Others will say that they get intrinsic rewards from performing a job well. The joy of completing a task that they set out to do is reward enough. They accept the trade and live with it.

Don't do it! You are simply creating a pattern that will be repeated. Remember, if you are trading some of your valuable time, make sure that the time you spend is dedicated to achieving your dreams.

Abundance Versus Scarcity

According to a tape I recently listened to by Dr. Steven Covey, author of *The Seven Habits Of Highly Effective People*, there are two attitudes about rewards: scarcity and abundance. Those who believe in scarcity will compete for what they view as a small prize. In other words, they believe that there isn't enough of the prize to go around, so they must get it before someone else does. For these people, the journey is not fun. They have not yet reached their goals, and they fear that while they are struggling, someone else may get the prize.

Those who believe in the theory of abundance realize that there are plenty of rewards for everyone. So, there is no race with others. In fact, they do not measure their success against the success of others. Abundance believers enjoy the journey because it is leading them to a goal that will be there when they have achieved enough to attain it!

Unfortunately, many businesses work on the scarcity principle. Employees do not share the wealth created within the company. Some top executives receive huge rewards while the majority of the employees scramble for the leftovers. People climb the ladder of success by competing with others.

If your place of employment works on the scarcity principle, you **MUST** make a change! Find a vehicle that will allow you to reap the rewards that you work so hard for. You can work with other people who are striving to change their economic lives and share in the rewards. There really is plenty to go around!

A Personal Note

It drives me crazy to give someone else power over my time. I have a great job, but I am always being asked to do things that simply do not provide me with any rewards. And, in this era of cost cutting, the university is simply not in a position to provide meaningful financial incentives.

So, aside from my job, I have my own business. It gives me rewards—both financial and intrinsic. I don't own my business because I want more work. I own it because I want more from life than ANY boss can give me.

When my employer gets a new idea that forces me to do more work for no reward, I channel the frustration into the motivation I need to build my own business. (By the way, I always seem to have plenty of motivation!)

Rule Number 8

"Offer Constructive Criticism"

> *The real art of conversation is not only*
> *to say the right thing in the right place,*
> *but to leave unsaid the wrong thing at the tempting moment.*
> —Dorothy Nevill

Censure, condemnation, disapproval, reproach—these are the words that my thesaurus gives as substitutes for the word "criticism." None of them sound very nice. Even when combined with the word "constructive," the meaning is still pretty nasty. I wouldn't want to receive constructive condemnation. Would you?

Yet, many of us feel a need to offer our opinions in order to make someone a better person. I do it. You probably have done it too.

The truth is that criticism is condemnation. No matter how we phrase it, we are telling someone that we disapprove of the way they did something. After criticizing them, we happily offer suggestions for doing it better. What gives us the right to do this? We naturally assume that we are in a position to demonstrate how effective we KNOW we can be.

The legendary comedian Hal Roach tells a great story to illustrate this point. A fellow named Casey won a motorcycle in a contest. He drove it to his rural village to show it off. His friend, O'Hara, hopped on the back, and the two set off through the country roads for a brisk ride.

After several miles, O'Hara yelled, "Stop, stop!" "What's the problem?" said Casey. "The wind is whipping into my chest something awful," complained O'Hara. "No problem," said Casey. "Take off your jacket, put it on backwards, and I'll button it up for you behind your back." "Great idea," said O'Hara.

The two jumped back on the motorcycle and raced along at high speed, with no complaints from the passenger. After a time, Casey realized that O'Hara was no longer sitting behind him. He turned his motorcycle around and headed back down the highway to look for his friend.

He soon came across O'Hara sitting in the middle of the road with a group of farmers standing around him. "Is he all right?" shouted Casey. "Well," replied one farmer, "he wasn't doing too badly when we first got here. But now that we've turned his head around, he has taken a turn for the worse."

The point of the story is that, all too often, people will go out of their way to say and do things that they think will help you—but end up hurting you in the process. Is that what we do when we criticize people? We think we are helping them when, in reality, we are emotionally turning their heads around.

Is Criticism Always Destructive?

According to Dale Carnegie's book *How To Win Friends And Influence People*, the answer is "YES." In fact, his admonition is in the very first chapter. The chapter's final words, found on page 17, are these: "Principle 1: Don't Criticize, Condemn or Complain."

When I found out that Dale Carnegie offered this as his first principle, I took notice. After all, this is the man who defined the art of getting along with others.

Being human, I don't always FOLLOW Mr. Carnegie's principles. But if he says it is right, I believe it with my whole being! He has taught thousands of people to make a better first impression and, more importantly, to extend that great impression throughout their relationships. That is power.

When you think about it, he is right. No one ever likes to receive criticism. When was the last time you were positively motivated by someone who criticized you? When was the last time criticism had a positive, rewarding effect on your life?

It was probably the time your boss showed you how to do something more efficiently. Maybe it was the time your spouse told you, in the most endearing way, that you could be a better driver if only you would ask for directions when you got lost. Perhaps you had that good feeling when your mother called you to say that people would respond to your law practice better if you only sat up straighter.

"Wait a minute," you say, "leave my mother out of this!" All right, I will, but offering constructive criticism is like assuming the role of a parent. You are saying, "Okay, little Jane/Johnny, here is how it SHOULD be done. It's for your own good."

Trading Places

Before offering any constructive criticism, put yourself in the other person's place. This is hard to do. We often forget about the other person. We are only concerned about what WE want. After all, that is usually why we offer criticism. We want something.

When was the last time that the recipient of your opinion asked you for it? How often does someone say, "Would you please condemn me?"

(Remember, "condemn" is one of the synonyms listed for "criticism" in the thesaurus.) Usually, the other person is looking for praise, not disapproval.

But we go around offering our heartfelt and sincere words of criticism. After all, there is work to be done, right? Well if the people we criticize had their way, they would do a better job if they got recognition and encouragement.

Let's take a typical example in business. Jane is a supervisor at a factory. Her shift is responsible for producing a certain number of widgets each hour. One of her employees, Jim, has been slow at taking the widget material out of the cartons and placing it on the line. Jane is afraid that she will not receive her bonus if the line does not speed up. Jim will not receive his bonus, either. But is Jim's bonus the reason that Jane offers constructive criticism to speed him up? Unlikely!

When Jane offers her suggestions for improving Jim's performance, he is not likely to accept it with open arms, jump for joy, and thank her for motivating him to achieve his full potential. He is more likely to resent the intrusion, keep it to himself, and possibly ignore her suggestions. It is just human nature.

It is one thing to criticize people in a job situation. If we confined our constructive comments to those situations, there would be no need for this chapter! However, we feel the urge to improve other people's lives in all sorts of relationships. We do it with our family at home, with our friends, and with our relatives. We just can't seem to help it.

How many millions of arguments between spouses have started when one person offers some constructive criticism to the other? More importantly, how many marriages have ended for the same reason?

The next time you feel the urge to offer advice, put yourself in the other person's place. Ask the question "Am I doing this to get something I want or to help the other person?" If the reason you take this action is to satisfy

YOUR needs, keep quiet. You won't accomplish your goals. You will only create resentment.

Is There An Alternative?

First, let me say that no one—not Dale Carnegie, not I, and not you—have gotten through life without criticizing someone else for something. There may even be times when the other person sincerely asks you for your help in modifying their behavior. There may be times when you really should help them by offering constructive criticism, for example, during a SCHEDULED performance appraisal at work. I can't say with absolute confidence that there will never be such a time.

What I am saying is that constructive criticism is almost always harmful. At best, it is less effective than showing appreciation for the GOOD things that other people do. Appreciation, not disapproval, wins the hearts and minds of others.

Successful leaders have always shown appreciation for their followers. This doesn't mean they simply thank their supporters. In fact, they do much more. They share the credit, show appreciation, offer rewards, and respond to the needs of those they work or live with.

If my words are not enough, let's once again look to Mr. Carnegie. Chapter 2 is titled "The Big Secret of Dealing With People." And what is the big secret? The chapter ends with this principle: "Principle 2: Show Heartfelt and Sincere Appreciation."

Carnegie covers this subject very well. Suffice it to say that the idea of praising someone's strong points is a much better way to evoke a positive response than to try to change his weaknesses.

As supervisors, teammates, parents, spouses, or others involved in relationships, we ASSUME that the other person does not know how to do the things we want them to do. In most cases, the other person

already knows how to do things better. **They just don't do it for some reason. So when we criticize them, it makes them mad. When we praise and appreciate them, it makes them happy. Which emotion is more likely to solve a problem?**

You can create winners by breaking the rule of offering constructive criticism. You win because you are not expending negative energy. Your partners win because they are not demeaned or condemned. You win again because people are less likely to criticize you. Wouldn't that be nice!?!

Try to imagine your relationships with other people as they SHOULD be. Will people want to be around you? Do they consider you a friend or an enemy of their self confidence? Will they be motivated to work with you or against you? To a great extent, YOU control the future of their feelings.

A Personal Note

Not criticizing people is just about the hardest challenge I face. Sometimes it seems like it's my job to criticize! However, I am learning.

I had an opportunity to practice what I preach a few weeks ago. My boss at the university had been under unusual pressure, and it was beginning to show around the office. This led to some negative feelings among the staff. My first inclination, as a senior faculty member, was to speak with a group of my colleagues and prepare a list of complaints for my boss' attention. I rationalized that we could point out the weaknesses he was displaying and get him to make some changes.

(continued on next page)

Then I realized it. I was about to violate my own principles! I was offering constructive criticism. The changes I wanted were not for the benefit of my boss. They were for me. His reaction would certainly have been negative.

What did I do? I decided I couldn't change my boss, I could only change ME. By taking positive steps, I could help control the outcome.

Instead of sitting on the sidelines, complaining and criticizing, I decided to do something. I offered my assistance with some of the extra work he was facing. This initiative showed him that I was willing to do more than simply pass judgment on his actions.

While this meant more work for me, the result was a better work place, with a more positive environment.

Skip the criticism. It won't get you the results you are looking for in the long run!

10 RULES to BREAK

Rule Number 9

"Accept Only Valid Excuses"

The difference between perseverance and obstinacy
is that one often comes from a strong will,
and the other comes from a strong won't.
—Henry Ward Beecher

There is a story about a man who goes to his neighbor's house and asks to borrow the lawn mower. The neighbor says, "I can't lend you my lawn mower, because my wife is making beef stroganoff tonight."

The man says, "What does your wife's cooking have to do with lending me the lawn mower?" "Nothing," says the neighbor. "But if I don't want to do something, then any excuse will do."

The point of the story is when you don't want to do something, you'll make an excuse so you don't have to do it! Isn't that true in all our lives?

Excuses are an interruption of the flow of whatever habits you have that lead to success. Unfortunately, excuses can move from the temporary realm to permanent status very quickly, because offering excuses can become habit forming. This temporary relief from responsibility may

become so comfortable that it turns into a permanent fixture of your behavior.

Priorities

People who make excuses let fear, laziness, or the desire for the status quo overcome their need to succeed. The power of the excuse—the relief from responsibility—is greater than the desire to achieve a dream. Achieving big dreams is the essence of self responsibility.

It is important—no, crucial—to have a prioritized sense of your life. Place your dream, and its achievement, first. Don't make excuses that violate the priorities in your life. Here is an example of how easily that can happen:

Harry wants to build a business. He chooses network marketing because it allows him the greatest freedom and flexibility. He can retain his primary job while building a business of his own. He knows that, with some work and effort now, he can achieve a lifestyle that few can even imagine. His greatest desire is to have time to spend with his family.

Yet, instead of getting out and sharing the opportunity with others, he spends five nights per week watching television. His excuse? He is too tired when he comes home from work. How can he get out of the house, be enthusiastic, and ask people to join him in a quest for a dream? He just doesn't have the energy.

This is Harry's excuse. It sounds plausible to him. In fact, like most people who make excuses, he believes that it is a VALID excuse. Is it?

Perhaps there are some nights when he really is exhausted. That's okay! It is all right to OCCASIONALLY give yourself a break. But Harry is allowing this situation to become permanent.

What can he do? Instead of watching television, Harry could read a book. Or, he could simply go to sleep after dinner and get up an hour earlier the next morning. In that hour, he could work on a list, meet someone for breakfast, exercise, or whatever. In other words, if Harry had his priorities straight, he would find some way of utilizing his time to achieve success.

Anything is possible if we have priorities. Anything.

"Anything Is Possible"—Are You Sure?

By this time, some reader is saying, "Well, I'll never run the four-minute mile." This is probably true, but do you really know? Have you ever dedicated yourself to the effort? When you were in your twenties, did you sacrifice everything else, spend day after day practicing, focus on this effort, and tell yourself, "I WILL DO THIS!?" Probably not.

The truth is that many of us really are not physically capable of heroic sporting achievements. But almost all of us are capable of achieving financial success. Certainly, if you are reading this book, you have the mental capacity to succeed. It is simply a matter of priorities.

Many doubters and skeptics will say, "Sure, I can succeed financially, but then I will never see my family. I'll be working all the time."

If you are saying, thinking, or feeling this, please realize that you are making an excuse. You are avoiding success because of some fear, no matter how noble the basis of that fear may be.

Stop making excuses. You can have it all!

Oh, The Excuses We Make...

Here are 10 excuses and a short rebuttal for each one. Do you recognize any of them?

1. I come from an underprivileged background.

That's too bad. Do you want your children to come from an underprivileged background too?

2. I want to focus on one thing at a time.

   Sure you do. Everyone does. But you need to do more than that today in order to succeed.

3. My kids are too little.

   Are they too little to see you work 50 hours a week for someone else's dream? Make the time and show them what a successful person looks like.

4. People like me will never succeed.

   You are absolutely right. Stop being a person like you and start being like successful people.

5. There aren't enough hours in the day.

   Then prioritize and get rid of the unimportant stuff.

6. There is a glass ceiling.

   Then start your own business. That way you won't have ANY ceiling.

7. The odds are against me.

   They certainly are. You better do something quickly to change them.

8. I'm too old to try anything new.

   If you really believe this, then you are right. What a shame. Your wisdom and experience could have helped us all. Rest in peace.

9. I'm too young to be taken seriously.

   If you really believe this, you are right. Too bad. Your spirit, excitement, and energy would have been refreshing. Grow up.

10. Things will be better next year.
    The definition of insanity—"Keep on doing the same things and expect the outcome to be different."

Perhaps you've used some of these excuses. Are they worth losing your dreams over? Are they valid? They will stand between you and what you really want out of life! Get rid of them!

A Personal Note

Since I am legally blind, I often attend conventions for the visually impaired so I can search for the latest technologies. Last year, I was invited to speak at one of these conventions, where I met Ted Henter. He was blinded in a motorcycle accident. He had developed a program that reads a computer screen out loud to blind people. Ted used the trade show at the convention to promote his excellent product. (In fact, I am using a screen reader right now as I write this book.)

Ted has vision. It is just not the physical kind. He sees opportunity where others see a road block. He has made no excuses. I admire that! And I, too, try to live my life without making excuses.

Rule Number 10

"Don't Mix Business with Pleasure"

---

*The secret of happiness is to do what you love to do,
and learn to love what you have to do to get there.*
—Dexter Yager

I used to believe the rule *Don't Mix Business with Pleasure* was right, and should be followed. That was in my younger days. I now understand that the idea that business can't be fun is quite immature.

Separating business from pleasure implies that business is something of a drudge. It projects the image of stern-faced, uptight people who don't smile. On the contrary, business is like a good game. It is to be enjoyed with people you respect and like.

I know that the saying *Don't Mix Business with Pleasure* originally applied to things like having parties with employees or subordinates, dating a colleague, and such. There are still standards that apply in this realm. Many companies have rules forbidding relationships between supervisors and employees. Whether it is unlawful or forbidden by policy, unprofessional conduct is improper. That is not the subject of this chapter.

So put aside the notion that pleasure deals with a naughty subject. Pleasure is fun! It can take all forms of expression. We are not dealing with "forbidden fruit." This part of the book is dedicated to innocent pursuits. Yet, most people are trained to consider all sorts of fun as unprofessional.

A few years ago, I was hired to be a motivational speaker on a four-day cruise. While any cruise is fun, I didn't want to go alone. Yet, if my wife accompanied me with our two small children, the resulting demands on our time could have been very stressful.

Our solution? We hired two babysitters and booked an extra cabin. They took my girls to the early dinner seating, while my wife and I enjoyed a late dinner with the clients. During the day, we were all able to enjoy the ship's activities. I had successfully combined business with pleasure.

Early Training

The concept that we must separate business and pleasure starts in early childhood. Children spend the first four years of their lives in play. They get up in the morning, eat breakfast, and start playing for the rest of the day. It is their job.

We expect them to learn something while playing. They increase their dexterity and learn socializing skills. They learn to be creative. They make things, paint things, and break things. It is their nature.

Kindergarten is often where children first understand that there is a difference between business and pleasure. Suddenly, their world becomes more structured. When they start elementary school, the structure really becomes entrenched. Students save their playtime activities for recess. While in school, "they are there to learn, not play!"

I put those words into quotations because I heard them over and over again when I was a child. Did you? Suddenly, the play and relaxation we enjoyed as children were put into restricted time slots. At recess, the pent-up energy was released in dramatic bursts. Traditionally, when children returned to the classroom, they were expected to listen intently, often without comment or question, while the teacher taught. We were trained, from an early age, to physically and mentally separate business from pleasure.

Grown-ups At School

As adults, we take the rules of elementary school and simply transfer them to our business lives. It is really amazing to consider. Imagine adult human beings being told when they can eat their lunch, who they can talk to, when to stop playing and start working, and so forth. Most people don't think about it. If they did, they would go crazy!

At work, we trade teachers for bosses. It would actually make sense for a boss to be a teacher. Good teachers teach us all they know. They want us to become as smart as they are. But hardly any bosses want us to know as much as they do. Why should they? If you knew what they know, you would be the boss. Where would that leave them?

Physicians tell us that the great majority of heart attacks occur on Monday mornings. Hardly anyone gets sick on Friday afternoons. A weekend sickness is considered a real tragedy. It destroys recess! We work hard all week so that the weekends can be the time for pleasurable pursuits. Just as in school, work and pleasure are strictly separated.

Working Pleasure

There are really two types of pleasure that can be derived from work. The first is the feeling of satisfaction from the work itself. The second type results from the rewards that the work provides.

You should enjoy what you do! Studies have shown that it is possible. Producing a useful product or a service that is appreciated by others can be enjoyable. Working with interesting people in a position of growth is also fun.

Unfortunately, many people find themselves in situations that are merely a grind. This is a shame, because work takes up so much of our lives. Most people spend at least one third of their waking hours at work.

There are five factors that can affect the pleasure we derive from work. They are as follows:

1. Time Flexibility. Most people have to PHYSICALLY be present at work during certain hours and certain days of the week. Even the owners of traditional businesses usually need to be present when their shops are open. If the owner is not there, the customers may not be served properly.

Break the rule: Create a work style that is not dependent on your physical presence at any given time. Enjoy work that can be performed anywhere, at any time, and that can be accomplished without your presence, if necessary. Free yourself from the time constraints that say, "You must work now, and keep working for eight hours."

2. The Work Itself. Many people are tired of their work. The challenge and excitement they once felt is no longer there.   Other people perform repetitive tasks. Some work is just plain unpleasant. On the other hand, some work is great—interesting, rewarding, and fun! It all depends on what you do.

Break the rule: Do something that helps other people and makes a difference in their lives. Do something that uses a combination of high tech and high touch to provide a service that is important to people. Do something that is worthy of your time and effort. Find work that is interesting, that changes every day, and provides you with challenges.

3. <u>The People.</u> This is a combination of colleagues, customers, and bosses. They can make the job fun or a real trial. Are these people positive influences where you work, or are they negative, grouchy, and complaining?

Break The Rule: Surround yourself with positive, caring people. This may sound difficult, considering the people you work with right now. It's not! There are environments that create positive people. Get going!

Imagine having a boss who helps you get what you want. Imagine a boss who acts as a mentor; teaching you to get more rewards and to become a better person. Imagine working with people who have your best interest at heart. This would certainly create pleasure at work.

4. <u>Rewards.</u> All work should provide meaningful rewards. Many rewards bring pleasure and satisfaction. They should be fun! They should be in direct proportion to the effort you put in.

Break The Rule: It is important to be rewarded for the work you do. Your business should provide rewards and incentives that are unlimited.

Rewards can be monetary or personal. Of course, the monetary rewards must come first. Many organizations try to substitute personal rewards, such as recognition or appreciation, for monetary rewards. Without sufficient money for work, the other rewards soon lose their effect.

Imagine work that has unlimited rewards and incentives. That's right, no limit. You can make as much as you would like. You can receive all the recognition you need. Everything you do that is positive will be rewarded. Wow!

This is what you need. Get a dream and then find a situation that combines a great business with the attainment of that dream. This is how you start designing your own destiny!

5. Ownership. This is different than empowerment. Empowerment is a buzz word in business today. It is a process in which your boss slowly relinquishes some control to you. The theory is that this allows you to "own" your job. It is a good start, but not NEARLY enough!

Owning an actual share of the business is essential. Being able to AFFECT the total outcome and PROFIT from it makes people productive and happy.

Break The Rule: You will not have control over your life until you own your business. Ownership lifts the barriers to personal fulfillment at work. If you own your business—especially if it's the RIGHT business—you can control all of the other factors affecting the pleasure you derive from work.

Combining Work And Pleasure

It is possible to combine work and pleasure. In fact, it is necessary for a healthy mental outlook. Most people work at least 40 hours per week. Allowing time for sleeping, this leaves only a short time for living. When the weekend arrives, most people rush through all of their personal chores so they can spend some time in pleasurable pursuits.

This creates stress. When the weather is bad, or something else happens to disrupt the precious weekend plans, it is very traumatic. This is even more critical during vacations.

Did you ever wonder what psychologists mean when they say, "Have a balanced life?" For the most part, they are referring to increasing your relaxation time by reducing the amount of time spent at work. How about another approach? Why not make WORK more pleasurable? Doesn't that make more sense?

Today, many businesses are ATTEMPTING to make the workplace more enjoyable. They offer flex-time, incentive packages, and the ability to do some work from home. "Non-traditional" network marketing businesses go one step further. Entire families can get involved with setting goals and enjoying the rewards of the work they perform. Husband and wife can travel all over the world to expand their business. That's mixing business with pleasure!

Pleasurable work that provides ample rewards will create balance in life. This reduces stress and increases good health.

Get The Firsthand Facts—Not The Secondhand Myths

You CAN mix business with pleasure. Remember, just because something has always been done a certain way does not make it the only way—or even the best way.

You've probably heard the story of the woman who always cut two inches off the end of a ham before she baked it. One day, her husband asked why she did this. "It's the way my mother did it," she explained. The husband decided to ask his mother-in-law the reason for this cooking method. She replied, "I have to cut the end off the ham because it's usually too long to fit into my baking dish." Like many myths we continue to hold true today, the reason for continuing this method was no longer valid!

Look at your situation objectively. It is a fact that you will live a healthier, happier life if you combine business with pleasure.

A Personal Note

When I first questioned the rule about mixing business with pleasure, I was shocked. It wasn't because the idea of separating business and pleasure was so appalling. It was because this rule was so pervasive. The idea that we so thoroughly shut off our emotions at work really did not make sense.

(continued on next page)

It wasn't until I thought about WHY we do this that I understood how the whole situation evolved. It started inschool! Remember the early training that we got there, where we separated "work" from "recess"? That's why my wife, Jeanne, and I put our children into a school that encourages interaction and fun while the students learn. I want our kids to grow up with the idea that it is possible to work and have pleasure simultaneously. I want them to develop a lifestyle that is fun and rewarding.

SECTION 2

---

10 RULES to MAKE

---

10 RULES to MAKE

10 RULES to MAKE

Overview

A Lesson From Our Children

One warm, spring afternoon, I took my two daughters to the playground. There were quite a few other kids there, although none of them seemed to know each other. It wasn't long, however, before they started playing a game of tag.

"Tag, you're it." said one little girl. "No," said the other, "this bench is the base." Before long, the kids had agreed to a few basic rules: Past the swing set was out of bounds. You couldn't tag the person who tagged you (they called it "no tag-backs"). Don't slap people—just *tag* them, and so on.

One boy suggested the rule that anyone could declare they were a base and, therefore couldn't be tagged. The group quickly threw out this rule. It made the game too difficult to play!

Eventually, through trial and error, the kids came up with a set of rules that made their game fun and challenging. They must have played for more than an hour—and everyone had a ball!

Life is like that game of tag the children organized—it's a great game when you choose the rules that work for you. If a rule works, if it helps you and others play the game better, then *make* that rule!

10 RULES to MAKE

Rule Number 1

Go Out and Claim
What Is Already Yours

---

*We are not weak if we make a proper use
of those means which the God of Nature
has placed in our power...The battle, sir, is
not to the strong alone, it is to the vigilant,
the active, the brave.*

—Patrick Henry

There is a humorous story about a man who built a home in a flood plain. His friends warned him not to build it there. "It will flood and you will drown," they said. "Don't worry," said the man. "The Lord will provide for me."

Not long after building his house, there was indeed a flood. As the waters rose, the man stood on the front porch, with the water around his knees. A boat came up to the house and the people in it shouted, "Get in the boat. Get in the boat."

"No, no," he replied. "The Lord will provide for me."

A few hours later, he was on the second floor, looking out the window at the rapidly rising water. A second boat arrived and again the people shouted, "Get in the boat. Get in the boat." Once again, he replied firmly, "No, no. The Lord will provide for me."

Eventually, the man stood on the roof, watching the rising waters swirl around his neck. A third boat came by. "Get in the boat. Get in the boat," they shouted. "No, no. The Lord will provide for me," the man replied.

The waters rose over his head and the man drowned.

He found himself standing in front of St. Peter at the Pearly Gates. "We didn't expect to see you here today," said St. Peter. "I certainly didn't expect to be here," said the man. "I thought the Lord would provide for me!"

St. Peter looked the man straight in the eye and said, "Fella, the Lord provided you with three boats and YOU DIDN'T GET IN!!!"

Like the man who built the house in the flood plain, we often WAIT for God, or someone else, to send us help. Yet, when we do receive it, we don't get in the boat! Is there a boat waiting for you right now? Have you put off doing something, waiting for EXACTLY the right moment? Get in the boat! And go out and claim what is already yours!

We have two incredible gifts. First, we have *unlimited personal development potential.* Second, our society is based on the beliefs of men and women who have guaranteed us *liberty.* Yet, neither of these gifts can achieve their maximum value unless they are fought for, claimed, and won. We cannot grow as humans, nor can we appreciate success, unless a price is paid. This chapter discusses the personal struggles we must each endure to claim our rights—and design our destinies.

Your Spiritual Birthright

For me, belief in a God is fundamental to full development as a human. Let me attempt to summarize my feelings and beliefs about God and His spiritual plan for people. Let me stress that these are MY beliefs. You may feel entirely differently. That is your right and does not invalidate either of our beliefs. I believe that:

> God created me in His image. He wants me to grow and achieve. I can serve Him by serving others. He does not intend for me to be controlled by any other man. I am an individual who must accept responsibility for my own future. I must design my own destiny, but can only accomplish it with the help of God.

I was not created to be delivered into slavery in any form. God wants me to be free. Only by achieving freedom can I completely serve others and, therefore, God. It is my God-given destiny to be free. It is a right and a future that I may lay claim to.

Yet, so many people seem to think that claiming their freedom is something that is contrary to God's will. Realize that you have been *given* freedom. You have it. It is yours to cherish and treasure.

Unfortunately, we spend much of our lives denying our human freedom. We become meek. We hope for a better day. We use the excuse that the Lord will provide for us, so we abdicate the role our personal input plays in our future.

Human Help

In order to claim what is already ours, we will probably need the help of others.

How can you identify people who are seriously able to help you claim what is already yours? There are some definite characteristics to look for. Your helper should:

> *Have a positive outlook on life.* Look for positive people. A negative person will only create negativity in you.

> *Have something to gain by helping you.* Remember, you want sustained, continued assistance. Only someone who has something to gain from your increased wealth and happiness will be interested in giving you honest and prolonged assistance.

> *Be successful himself.* Look for successful people. Don't take advice from someone who has failed in life. Would you ask a divorced person to help save your marriage? Do you seek parenting advice from someone whose children are in jail? Of course you don't. Yet we continually listen to people who are broke when they give us advice on achieving wealth.

Look for the right people to help you. Some of the people in position to offer help have not taken care of their own lives first. Steer away from false prophets!

What Can You Claim?

Claim your freedom. It is simple. You live in a free society. You have free will. Make the choice, get help and stick with it.

Here are a few things to claim:

Early retirement—Why should you work until age 65? Why not retire early, very early? Claim it!

Control of your life—Why should you let a boss tell you what to do, every day of your life, for the rest of your life? Be independent. Claim it!

Financial security—The average family is only 90 days from being broke. Why should that be? There are a lot of wealthy people in the world. There is absolutely no reason why you should not be one of them. Claim it!

Good health—No one can guarantee you good health. However, you can improve your health by lowering stress. And money is often the only thing that stands between you and the best medical care. Claim it!

Education—Do you want your children to have the very best education? Will they have all the choices they want? You can give them anything money can buy if you are only willing to create wealth. Claim it!

Freedom of choice—Choose your home, the places you live, the times of year you vacation, and so on. It is there for the brave, the strong, and the resolute. Claim it!

Think big and achieve big—Enjoy the full fruits of the marvelous world God created. Enjoy the full victory of freedom that was guaranteed by great men and women who gave their lives to freedom's cause. To settle for less is to deny their faith in you.

The Welfare Dilemma

As I am writing this book, there is a great debate over welfare reform in the United States. Currently, there are many third- and fourth-generation welfare families. It was supposed to be a safety net—a temporary assistance to those who need it. Yet the lack of incentives, and the federal government's bureaucratic approach to the situation, have made welfare a lifetime of free handouts for thousands of UNDESERVING people.

This is not a political book, and the discussion about welfare is not meant to be political. However, the situation does provide an excellent example of how the wrong people can deliver a terrible message to those who need their help.

If welfare is supposed to be a temporary situation, then it stands to reason that the government wants to help people get off welfare and into productive work. That makes sense. But look who the government sends to help poor people become financially secure. The government sends social workers. Let me explain.

I teach at a university where we train business people in the college of business, and social workers in the College of Health and Professional Studies. The people who study social work are, for the most part, sincere, helpful, and well-intentioned. They have a burning desire to serve others. Unfortunately, these wonderful people are not trained to create wealth, nor are they given an incentive to do so.

Undoubtedly, the people on welfare have problems other than financial ones. They need a shoulder to cry on, and someone who can improve their relationships with their children and spouses. However, NONE of these forms of assistance gets people off welfare.

And what about the poor social workers? I use the word "poor" because that aptly describes the amount of money they are paid. The social workers have huge case loads of poor, problem-ridden clients. What is the incentive for a social worker to get someone off welfare? There is none. Suppose you were a social worker, and among all the cases you have, there are a few who show some spark, some interest, and some talent for getting their lives together. What happens if you actually help them get off welfare?

They are replaced with someone else! In other words, your case load remains the same. Now, however, you have one less client who had some hope. The chances are good that the hopeful, hard-working client is replaced by someone who has no desire to make a dramatic change in his life. What a terrible deal!

And what do the welfare recipients think about the social workers? I can't say for sure, but consider this comparison. The welfare recipient doesn't have children in day care, doesn't have to drive to work, gets a subsidy for housing, receives free food, and is free to stay at home all day. The social worker does just the opposite and doesn't make much more money than his clients!

The only thing that will get people off welfare is to give them a REASON to get off it! We must then give them a MEANS to get off it!

Here is my plan. Let's assume that it costs $20,000 per year to keep someone on welfare. Why not give the social workers a $5,000-per-year bonus for everyone they get off welfare? Now, who would want to be a social worker? Lots of people. And, they would insist on receiving sound business training to help prepare people financially for the responsibilities of work.

Soon, you would have rich people teaching poor people how not to be poor. (Today, we have underpaid people teaching poor people how not to be poor.)

Welfare recipients won't just magically become excited about going to work. After all, why should they make money for the social workers? So, use a system like network marketing that fosters individual creative free enterprise. Instead of giving them a handout, give them the possibility for a hand up!

Let's Get Personal

How does this whole welfare scenario apply to you? After all, you aren't on welfare. Or are you? Are you planning on using Social Security to cover some of the costs of your retirement? Do you really think it will be there when you retire?

Who are your mentors, leaders, and helpers? Will your friends, who are moderately successful, be able to help you when your company has a massive layoff? Will they pay your mortgage or your children's education bills?

We decry and criticize the welfare system. Yet, in so many ways, we are sticking our heads in the sand, accepting what we have instead of taking the steps to claim what is ours to claim—financial security and freedom.

Look for successful people who can help you. Don't let someone affect your life if they have not taken care of the needs of their own family. Live a positive life, surrounded by positive people, and go out and claim what is already yours!

A Personal Note

As an American, I am grateful to the men and women who were brave enough to claim freedom for themselves, and who passed that freedom on to me. Now it is my turn.

Will I reclaim that freedom for myself? I am trying. Political and economic forces are continually rising that limit my ability to design my destiny. Yet, I know that by visualizing a dream, and working in a system to achieve that dream, I can succeed.

My personal freedom and liberty are only the beginning of the challenge. Like the signers of the Declaration of Independence, I struggle to give my children—and their children—the freedom they deserve. I know that their chances for success depend directly upon my example.

When I sometimes falter, I think of my children, and my commitment builds. They deserve what past generations have given me—not just the CHANCE to succeed, but a role model for claiming all that life holds for those who seek to claim it!

10 RULES to MAKE

Rule Number 2

Get the Whole Story

Minds are like parachutes.
They only function when they are open.
—Attributed to
Sir James Dewar

Have you ever heard the joke about the dim-witted man who wanted to start a chicken farm? Three times he bought a batch of baby chicks. Each time, they all died. He wanted some help, so he contacted the local state agricultural university and spoke to a noted professor.

"My chickens all die before they grow up," said the farmer.

"I'm surprised," said the professor. "This is a great area for raising chickens. I'll send you some of our newly developed food. Then call me in another month."

A month went by. The farmer called the professor again. "The chickens are still not growing," said the farmer, "even with the new food. Do you think I'm planting them too deep or too close together?"

The moral of this tale: *Get the Whole Story* before you make a recommendation or decision.

Like the professor, we often make decisions before we get all the facts. We may even dismiss opportunities, either because of what we THINK we know, or because of rumor, hearsay, or innuendo. When making decisions, use DUE DILIGENCE.

What Is Due Diligence?

Due diligence is a pseudo-legal term that implies it is up to the researcher to find out all the facts. Unfortunately, due diligence is often viewed as a negative factor. It shouldn't be.

A reasonable person should attempt to look fairly at all opportunities. Under due diligence, business people attempt to discover both the pros and cons of situations. Certainly, this may include input from friends, family members, and business associates. However, this information should not be weighed as heavily as firsthand knowledge gained from highly credible sources.

A good friend of mine was looking at a network marketing opportunity. He attended a meeting where a successful individual explained the business. Other successful people, including some of his friends, were also present at the meeting.

He then entered into some research of the company, using what he claimed was due diligence. How did he carry out the information search? He went to the World Wide Web on his computer. "Oh," he told me, "at least 20 people have said negative things on the Internet about this concept. I told you it was a terrible idea!"

That man was willing to ignore the facts because 20 strangers told him it was a bad idea. This wasn't due diligence. It was an excuse not to do anything.

Relax...And Listen

There is an old saying, "God gave us two ears and only one mouth. Take this hint and LISTEN twice as much as you talk." We will never get the whole story if we constantly interrupt people. If we give voice to our doubts before the other person has had the opportunity to present all the relevant facts, we will probably miss the opportunity.

It is important to separate the SEARCH FOR INFORMATION from the DECISION PROCESS. There is plenty of time to make a decision. We usually don't allow enough time to gather the information.

As a marketing professor, I am familiar with the process people go through when buying a product. Generally, marketers agree that there are five steps consumers take when making a purchase. (I've taken the liberty of changing the words a little to make it easier to remember.) The five steps are below:

1. There's something I need. (Problem Recognition)
2. How do I get it? (Information Search)
3. Identify alternatives. (Alterative Evaluation)
4. Now that I've found it, do I buy it? (Purchase Decision)
5. Keep it or return it? (Post-purchase Evaluation)

We all go through these stages for each decision we make as consumers. How long we spend in each stage depends on the type of product and the amount of commitment it requires. For example, buying a loaf of bread requires far less thought than purchasing a new business.

We will look at these five stages from two perspectives. First, as a buyer, you should understand how it is necessary to go through all five of these stages in order to hear the whole story. Second, as a business person, you need to understand that people require a REASON to hear the whole story. If they do not have a compelling drive to listen to you, they will simply tune you out!

1. There's something I need.

People will not change unless they realize there is a need for change. The definition of problem recognition is "when a desired state is different than the actual state." For example, when you want to have a Mercedes in your garage, and there isn't one, then you have problem recognition.

When we want people to take some action, it is first necessary to help them realize that they may not have what they could have. This is their problem recognition.

In this book, we talk about the power of a dream. Having a dream is a form of problem recognition. Without a dream and, subsequently, goals, it is impossible for humans to commit to the changes necessary to succeed.

The first step in getting someone to hear the whole story is to help them realize what they want. Secondly, we must show them that they can get what they want. Then they will take the next step.

2. How do I get it?

Only after someone realizes that what they want is not what they have will they go on an information search. Too often, marketers of all kinds try to give people information before the client wants it or cares about it.

If you are sharing an opportunity with someone and they don't seem to be interested in the information you have, it may be because they have not yet realized that a problem exists. Go back to the dream. Get them excited about the POSSIBILITIES first, then show them how they can "get it."

Most people operate under the "What's in it for me?" system. They will not seek information unless they can reasonably expect that the search will yield some solution to their problems. And they will not seek a solution unless they first recognize that a problem exists.

3. Identify alternatives.

It is highly unlikely that there is only ONE solution to any problem. Of course, there is often one BEST solution to most problems. However, TELLING someone what the best solution is can be vastly different from having them DISCOVER it. Allow people to sample the possibilities.

Most people hate to make mistakes. They don't want to commit to something only to discover that there could have been a better choice. Sampling allows people to make the best decision. This can take many forms.

Most ice cream parlors will provide their customers with free samples of the flavors. Not many people are brave enough to buy a brand new flavor without tasting it first. The next time the sales person tells you about the new banana-nut-ripple-twist-fruit-parfait-breadfruit frozen yogurt, will you ask for a sample before you buy it? Of course! You don't want to waste your time or money on a product that may not meet your needs.

How can people sample a business opportunity? Let them see the results. Take them to meet people who have been successful in the same business opportunity. Let them know it can work for them.

4. Now that I've found it—do I buy it?

Generally, people do not make the decision to commit to something until they have recognized the problem, gathered some information, sampled the alternatives, and prepared themselves for the decision. This can happen very quickly, or it can take months. It depends on the person and the opportunity.

Some people, like me, make purchase decisions rather quickly. Others, like my wife, require much more time to consider everything. While this tends to drive me a little crazy, we make our major decisions together.

At any rate, the purchase decision will only occur after the person decides that this solution is the best one for their problem. Don't expect a decision until that time.

5. Keep it or return it?

Almost all humans have second thoughts after a major purchase. It's called "buyer's remorse." Did you ever buy a car and, on the way home, wonder if you bought the best one for you? It's natural.

When sharing a business opportunity with someone, realize that they will have some post-purchase anxiety. This is a very fragile time. It may not take much for someone else to destroy the belief that they made the right decision. A neighbor, spouse, family member, or friend can dislodge their belief in themselves and the opportunity.

If you have used due diligence, and heard the whole story, then have confidence in yourself. You are capable of making a good decision. You did not get this far in life by being completely crazy! (We will talk about being a little crazy in another chapter. A little craziness is good!)

If you are helping someone to develop a business opportunity, work with them as they struggle with post-purchase evaluation. If necessary, repeat the steps. Go back to problem recognition—their dream. It is the dream that drives them through the problems they will inevitably face.

Get them plugged into a system of information and dream building. Let them go through the information search again. The information search will reinforce their beliefs. REMEMBER, THEY WILL BE LETTING IN NEGATIVE INFORMATION FROM MANY OTHER SOURCES. KEEP THEM UP TO THEIR EYEBALLS IN A POSITIVE STREAM OF INFORMATION!

Finally, allow them to sample success. Do some positive dream building. Hold their hand while they get their business started.

Parting Thoughts

Opportunities are sometimes delivered into our laps, but unless we are ready to hear about them we will not get the whole story. Make the effort to research, gather reliable and credible information, and make decisions for your financial future based on due diligence.

In order to ensure your success, you will have to help others get the whole story. Start with the problem recognition by building a dream with them. Any time there is need for more input, start and end with the dream.

For each person, the "whole story" will be different. Help them make it THEIR story. Each of us would like to write the script for our lives. So, when helping people hear the "whole story," give them a beginning, sometimes even a middle. But, allow them to create the ending. It will be much more compelling if they create the last chapter themselves!

A Personal Note

This is the seventh book I have written. Along the way, I have learned a valuable lesson about writing books: Write them for the benefit of the reader, nothing else. It wasn't until my sixth book, *Reclaiming The American Dream,* that I figured this lesson out. My first five books were written so that people could do their *jobs* better. That wasn't personal enough. It didn't solve any problems for them—only for their bosses.

Hopefully, you are a little quicker than I in learning this lesson. When giving someone the whole story, give them a reason to listen to it. Make it personal. Share some personal experiences, but don't make it your story. It is their time to write a few chapters.

10 RULES to MAKE

Rule Number 3

Become UN-equal

The idea that men are created free and equal
is both true and misleading; men are created different;
they lose their social freedom and their individual autonomy
in seeking to become like each other.

—David Riesman

We hold these truths to be self evident, that all men are created equal, that they are endowed by their Creator with certain unalienable rights, that among these are life, liberty, and the pursuit of happiness. —U.S. Declaration of Independence

These words are the foundation of democracy. Despite these words, I am urging you to become UN-equal. Why? Because being equal means being average. The average person in America is poor, or at least in financial danger. Do you want to be average? I don't!

Equality Of Opportunity

In the United States, we are guaranteed the opportunity to pursue our dreams. Everyone has the same opportunity. But not all men will take advantage of the equal opportunity that they have. People may say that they are underprivileged, that they come from a poor background. Indeed, these factors can pose a serious problem. SO WHAT! Using this as a reason for not achieving your dreams is simply an excuse.

We are all guaranteed the right to PURSUE our happiness. We are not guaranteed success. The men and women who fought the American Revolution did not ask for a guarantee. They simply wanted opportunity. They knew if they could only remove the blockade to their freedom of choice, they could achieve their largest dreams.

Over the last 200 years, we have steadily traded our rights to freedom of opportunity for security. We have developed social programs that redistribute wealth and penalize those who make and create wealth. In an effort to guarantee equality of opportunity, we have instead created equality of achievement.

What Is Equality Of Achievement?

Opportunity is different than achievement. Opportunity means that we can freely make choices that will lead to success. Achievement is the attainment of success. Our government has confused the two. Welfare, Social Security, and other programs attempt to relieve people of the responsibility for achievement. Under welfare, whether or not citizens make an effort to achieve, they will receive payments for the good fortune of living in a democracy.

This guarantee of achievement without effort tends to reduce or eliminate incentives. Why work when the government will take care of you anyway? Of course, the intentions of the people who created this legislation were honorable. They wanted people to have a certain standard of living. However, the results have been extraordinarily depressing.

Achievement should result from effort. And that effort should naturally be rewarded financially. Achievement will not be attained by everyone,

but, at least in this country, achievement CAN be attained by virtually anyone.

Will some people have to work harder than others? Yes. Will some people have to overcome physical handicaps in order to achieve their dreams? Yes. Will some people have to overcome poor family backgrounds, disastrous neighborhoods, prejudice, and bigotry in order to achieve? Yes. It doesn't matter what your circumstances are. In order to achieve your dreams, you will have to become UN-equal. You will have to do what others are unwilling to do.

Equal Is Average

If you merely want equality, your goals are too low. Consider some of these facts about the AVERAGE person:

> The average family has nearly $4,000 in credit card debt.

> According to the Department of Health, Education and Welfare, the average person will have a retirement income of $7,500 per year in today's money.

> According to *Money* magazine, the average American will not be able to stop working when he or she reaches retirement age.

> The average person will work for someone else for almost 50 years of his life.

> The average person has no ownership interest in the company he works for.

So, do you want to be average, or do you want to be UN-average? Do you want to be equal to everyone else, or do you want to be UN-equal?

Most people are afraid to be UN-equal. It is much easier to remain average. If you are average, you will have plenty of company. There is an old saying, "Misery loves company." It is true. Somehow, it doesn't seem so bad when all of your friends are in the same financial condition you are.

For many people, the idea of becoming UN-equal raises moral questions. They can't understand how they can be UN-equal and still be a good person. They mistakenly believe that UN-equality means that they will look down on others. They assume that an UN-equal person will create his achievement by hurting others. Yes, some people do this. But, it doesn't have to be that way.

The Burning Platform (A True Story)

Not many years ago, a terrible fire broke out on an oil rig in the North Sea off the coast of Scotland. Many lives were lost. One man who did survive told a remarkable story that has great impact for anyone who seeks to overcome challenges to achieve a goal.

At the height of the inferno, this man stood on a platform 150 feet above the surface of the frigid water. He had a choice. He could either jump off the platform into the water below, or stay and perish in the fire. If he survived the jump, he would still have only a slim chance to live long enough in the freezing sea to be rescued. He knew, however, that staying on the platform would certainly kill him.

He jumped, landed safely among the debris, and was rescued. Many of his friends stayed on the platform and were killed.

What is the moral of this story? He became UN-equal. The average person died in the fire. He took extraordinary measures and lived. Each man on that oil rig had an equal opportunity. Only a few had an unequal outcome.

Like the man who jumped from the burning tower, achievement is a decision. We either decide to achieve or we decide to remain equal. If you decide to become UN-equal, do you automatically change your basic character and moral beliefs? Of course not. If you were a good average person, you will be a good above-average person. Success will not change you. In fact, it will help you to help others.

The secret is to become UN-equal by helping others to become UN-equal. Then, after you have become UN-equal, continue to help others to achieve their dreams.

Five Steps To Becoming UN-equal

There are essentially five things you must do in order to become UN-equal. They are simple steps, yet they are difficult. There is the possibility that you might fail. Fortunately, if you make the right decisions, even failure to achieve your largest dreams will not allow you to fall into the "average" ranks again.

In other words, the efforts you made to reach your bigger dreams will elevate you above your former level! Like the old saying goes, "If you reach for the stars, you'll at least clear the fence!"

Once you have begun the journey toward becoming UN-equal, it is unlikely that you will ever be satisfied with equality again.

Step 1. *Visualize and get a dream.*

Defining your dream is so fundamentally important to becoming UN-equal that it bears mentioning here again. The average person does not have a dream. He has traded it for security and reality. Most people don't dare to dream because they are afraid of becoming disappointed and bitter.

The UN-equal person has a huge, strong, compelling dream. He uses the dream to drive himself. Instead of shrinking his dream to meet reality, he expands his reality to achieve his dreams.

Step 2. *Find a system.*

In order to become UN-equal, you will either have to invent a system for creating wealth or find one that already exists. Here is a big clue: Getting a good education, getting a job, and working hard are not the systems you need to become UN-equal. Those are the systems for becoming average.

Look for a system that has all the elements already in place for creating extraordinary results. A proper system should have reliable, guaranteed, and popular products and services, unlimited rewards, a powerful incentive system, and equal opportunity for everyone. Don't be fooled by "get-rich-quick" schemes. You should only be rewarded for helping yourself—and others—create wealth.

Step 3. *Find a mentor.*

A mentor is someone who can help you to become UN-equal. The ideal mentor is someone who is already UN-equal. This doesn't mean that he is wealthy. It means that your mentor should be on the road to financial success—a person who has made the decision to become UN-equal.

The best mentor is one who will have something to gain if you become successful. Look for an UN-equal person who will benefit if YOU become UN-equal.

Step 4. *Grow.*

You need to change. If you are successful, with all the money and time in your life that you will ever need, if you have a guaranteed, residual income stream that can be willed to your children, if your family and moral values are already strong, if you are an excellent leader and all your relationships are thriving, then you do not need to grow. If you are like the rest of us mortals, then you need to grow and change in order to succeed.

It stands to reason that if you had already made all the changes in your life that you needed, then you would already be successful. If you do not have what you really want, then you have to change in order to get it.

If this is so apparent, then why do most people ignore the need for personal growth and change? BECAUSE THEY ARE ALREADY EQUAL AND AVERAGE! It doesn't require any growth or change to stay where you are!

Read books, listen to tapes, get involved with motivated people, and grow. The average American doesn't really learn anything after he finishes school. And, unfortunately, they do not teach personal growth in school. They teach only skills, not how to get along with others.

Step 5. *Help others to become UN-equal.*

The best way to start is by helping others to find their dreams. After all, in order to become UN-equal, they will have to go through the same steps you did. Remember, everyone is equal at the start. Only a few are UN-equal in the end. You will want to have some UN-equal friends, so it is a good idea to help them!

Kindness, love, understanding, support, and a lack of willingness to accept excuses will help others to achieve. Of course, you won't be able to do this until you have first grown to the point where you have the CAPABILITY to help. Your personal growth will make it possible for others to achieve their dreams.

Parting Thoughts

Becoming UN-equal does not mean that you will become unfair. On the contrary, it will require you to grow, change, and probably become a better person. The only other choice is to remain average.

Average people are at the mercy of their bosses, the government, and anyone else who can afford to tell them what to do. Average is not good. It is only tolerable because so many people are stuck there with you.

Follow the leaders who have become UN-equal. If you choose your mentor carefully and become part of a success system, you can grow, change, and prosper. You will become UN-equal and will have the opportunity to help friends, family, and loved ones become UN-equal as well.

A Personal Note

I am writing this chapter on July 3rd. Tomorrow is the anniversary of the signing of the American Declaration of Independence. I love that document. In fact, I read it often.

In grade school, when I first was exposed to the Declaration, it really didn't mean much to me. Even though I grew up in Philadelphia, the real meaning of the Declaration escaped me until I began to explore the meaning of the free enterprise system established in 1776.

The signers of the Declaration wanted everyone to have opportunity. They declared that all men are equal. I take that declaration seriously. Yet, I know that the equality that each of us has is only an equality of opportunity. I believe that it is my personal responsibility to seize that opportunity. I know that if I do, I will become UN-equal.

Being UN-equal is a privilege. It carries with it the responsibility to help others achieve. On this eve of Independence Day, I am extremely grateful for those who risked everything to guarantee my equality of opportunity, and I will take the responsibility to make the most of it.

---

10 RULES to MAKE

Rule Number 4

It's Better to Own Half a Watermelon Than a Whole Grape

I would rather have 1 percent of the efforts of one hundred men than 100 percent of the efforts of one man.
—J. Paul Getty

It was my father's cousin, Harry, who first introduced me to this rule. Uncle Harry was a stockbroker with a seat on the New York Stock Exchange. He often advised clients who were going public or thinking about selling shares in their business to raise money. Many of the clients were reluctant to relinquish control of their companies. I was one client who had such misgivings. (Of course, I asked Uncle Harry for free advice.)

He asked me, "Would you rather own half a watermelon or a whole grape?" This question stuck with me through the years. It makes sense!

Too often we try to control, dominate, and own the whole operation. Because we do that, we thwart the company's ability to grow. Instead,

it remains small. **Yes, we have control, but of a very small product, service, or organization.**

Uncle Harry had the right idea. Involve other people, give them a piece of the action, and prosper from their effort.

Thank you for the advice, Uncle Harry!

Triumph Of The Nerds

For a great, modern, high-tech example of this principle, watch the PBS series called *Triumph of the Nerds*. It is a six-hour series that chronicles the rise and fall of computer giants such as Bill Gates, Steve Jobs, and others. Their stories perfectly illustrate the process of owning half a watermelon rather than a whole grape.

The story is about Microsoft, Apple, and IBM. Each of these companies played a major part in the development of the personal computer. Yet, the way that each company (or more specifically, the major players) handled their quest determined the winners and losers.

When IBM decided to enter the personal computer world, there were very few competitors. A few companies had begun to sell office equipment that vaguely resembled today's machines. But the emphasis was completely on products for the office—not the home.

IBM began to search for a company to develop the operating system for its machines. IBM contracted with Microsoft to build the Disk Operating System (DOS).

Early in the process, Gates, of Microsoft, made one of the greatest business decisions in modern history. He decided to create a system that would run on nearly ANY machine. He licensed IBM, and many competitors, to use the system in their computers.

Microsoft did not try to corner the market on computers. Instead, it wanted to have a small piece of each computer that was sold, everywhere. IBM, on the other hand, tried to control its market by keeping its machine components to itself.

About the same time, Steve Jobs created the APPLE. It was a great machine. Many people claimed that it was easier to operate than the IBM and its many clones. Unfortunately, because Apple would not license any of its engineering, no other company produced equipment using the Apple technology. This meant that the amount of software available for the Apple was also limited.

Soon, it became very easy to purchase software that would run on DOS. On the other hand, the Apple software was limited to some specialized functions. Microsoft began to grow, making Bill Gates the world's richest man.

The real death blow for Apple came when Microsoft released Windows™ software. Now, even IBMs could run as smoothly and as easily as the graphics-driven Apples. And, once again, Bill Gates licensed the use of the software to anyone who had a reasonable use for it. His half a watermelon was now gigantic. Apple's whole grape was shrinking into a raisin.

And what about IBM? The giant corporation was forced to close plants and lay off about 80,000 people. It didn't share the wealth, and it suffered greatly for it. This is not to say that IBM is endangered. It is still a major force in technology and an American icon. However, its position would have been vastly improved under a different strategy.

Share And Grow

We are all taught to share. When you were playing in the sandbox, who was more popular—the one who shared or the one who tried to put all the toys in his corner? We know that sharing is right, yet, as we grow older, we try to develop our independence, refusing to share with others.

Stephen Covey discusses this progression in his book *The Seven Habits Of Highly Effective People*. He says that we should move through three stages: dependence, independence, and interdependence. Unfortunately, most people get stuck in the independent stage.

As children, or when we are new in business, we are dependent on others. As children, we depend on our parents. They tell us what to do, care for us, and make sure we don't get hurt. As adults, many people find this same security. They belong to a union that helps them to be treated fairly. Or they have a boss who tells them what to do. For most people, this is an unhappy situation, but they put up with it because it gives them security.

As we grow, we become increasingly independent. Teenagers buy a car, get a job, and spend more time on their own. The same thing happens in the workplace. Some people seek independence. They may open a business of their own where they are the boss and their destiny is in their own hands.

People in the independent stage must make a choice. They can either remain independent, owning a whole grape and being indispensable, or they can mature even further into the interdependence stage. They help others to develop. They become replaceable. As their business and wealth grow, they become more free.

It requires great personal growth to become interdependent. You must learn to: (1) relinquish control, (2) depend on others, and (3) share the wealth with them. Sound scary? Well, the good news stems exactly from these three points.

First, you are no longer in control of every single detail of the operation. You are now free to concentrate on the larger picture. You can GROW your business because you are not bogged down in the details. You don't sweat the small stuff!

Second, many highly independent people find it very difficult to depend on others. However, the interdependent person understands the limitations of being independent. For example, independent people cannot be duplicated. They are the only ones who can do what they do.

Interdependent people have made themselves duplicatable. They want ANYONE to be able to do what they do. They want to work closely with others, using the combined efforts of everyone to create more than any of them could have managed on their own.

Third, as you learn to depend on others, you will learn to reward them for their effort. This should come in the form of profit sharing. Profit and equity sharing give others an incentive to further develop YOUR success.

True profit sharing stems from a commitment to create personal incentives through an allocation of rewards based on individual effort. Many companies try to utilize team rewards for profit sharing. This is relatively worthless, because it places limits on the individual.

On the other hand, interdependence does not mean that we get lost in the group. It means that individuals work together to achieve their own mutual benefits. The individual's rewards are not limited by, or dependent upon, the work of the group. Rather, each person contributes input and receives a share of the outcome proportional to his efforts.

In short, as John Naisbait predicted in *Megatrends,* these highly effective people are working in NETWORKS!

The Network Concept

In a network, individuals provide each other with help so that personal goals can be met. A journalist recently told me that she was writing a story on people who had been laid off from large corporations and were now working in "non-traditional" jobs. She had no idea how to find some of these people to interview them. She eventually went to the Internet and posted a request for volunteers on a computer bulletin board. Dozens of responses arrived. She would have never discovered these people without this network.

In a network company, each individual is interdependent on others. It is not possible to build a huge business while acting independently. That will only carry the distributor so far. Interdependence makes the distributor replaceable and duplicatable. It increases his wealth by allowing each person to contribute and receive rewards proportionally.

Build your network and receive the benefits produced by others who are working for your success while they achieve their own. In fact, surpass the advice of J. Paul Getty. Get one percent of the efforts of not 100, but 1,000, men. That creates wealth!

A Personal Note

I have made a real effort to move through the three stages discussed by Dr. Covey. As a child, I was dependent on my family and friends. Later, as a young adult, I worked hard to create my independence. I didn't want help from anyone. I was my own man. It was my way or the highway. What a rugged individualist I became. Proud, unbending, free! (Or so I thought.)

Then I got married. What a shock! At first, Jeanne and I retained our independent ways. Gradually, however, we began to develop interdependence. My life is richer because of it. And, as we learn to work together in business, along with other people, our lives have become WEALTHIER as well.

10 RULES to MAKE

Rule Number 5

Make Some Bad Decisions

Anything worth doing is worth doing poorly,
until you learn to do it well.
                                        —Zig Ziglar

So now you're really confused. You are saying, "There must be a misprint here. Shouldn't this rule, *Make Some Bad Decisions*, be a rule to break?" It certainly seems that way on the surface. What kind of writer would give you advice to make some BAD decisions? I would!

There is an old story about a hound dog that was howling late at night. He woke up a farmer and his wife. The wife was very disturbed and said to her husband, "Go out and see what is making that crazy dog carry on so much."

The man barely stirred and said, "Oh, Ma. I'm just too tired to move."

The howling continued for another hour and again, the woman begged the man to go see what was making the dog moan. Again, he gave the same answer.

"Oh, Ma. I'm just too tired to move."

So the howling went on. Finally, for the third time, the woman ordered the man to investigate. And, for the third time, he gave his patent answer.

"Oh, Ma. I'm just too tired to move."

So, the woman got out of bed, put on her shawl and went out into the night. Suddenly the howling stopped. When the wife returned to bed, the man asked, "What was wrong with that stupid dog?"

"He was lying on a thorn bush," said the woman. "He was just too tired to move."

How many people do you know like that dog—people who would rather howl and complain than change their position? How many people do you know like the husband—people who would rather suffer and wait for someone else to solve their problems instead of taking the initiative to do it themselves? Are you one of them?

Too Tired To Move

Some people are just too lazy, too afraid, or too un-motivated to make a decision, EVEN WHEN THEY CLEARLY NEED TO DO SOMETHING IN THEIR LIVES! Like the dog on the thorn bush or the man in the bed, they would rather put up with the pain in their lives than make some changes.

I have met too many good people who know they should be doing something. Yet, these intelligent folks will put up with the pain of their current existence rather than taking action. They say, "I have already tried making changes. It didn't work for me." They have become old before their time. Yes, they are too tired, but they are tired only because they have stopped trying.

There are three types of fatigue that plague humans: physical, mental, and spiritual. Each of them can be very real. Fortunately, each of them can be easily cured.

Physical fatigue—Now, there may be an underlying health reason for physical tiredness. I am not suggesting that I know how to cure an ailment that only a doctor should treat. However, a great deal of physical fatigue is caused by the everyday stress of life. It is curable, but only through action.

In many cases, the causes of the tiredness can be overcome with money. Isn't that amazing? A simple thing like money can alleviate so many problems. For instance, the single mother who has to get her children up in the morning, take them to day care or school, work all day, and then return home to cook and clean is probably very tired. However, if she had enough money to hire a cleaning person and a cook, that would make a huge difference in her life.

Many two-parent families find themselves in the same boat. They are both working, not because they WANT to work, but because they must both work to support the family and pay the bills. Wouldn't more money make a HUGE difference in their lives? Of course it would. They could hire others to do some of their work. Or one parent could stay home full time.

Mental fatigue—This is often caused by the same problems. Stress and overwork combine to reduce mental capacity. People get in a terrible rut. They become so mentally exhausted that they are no longer able to recognize opportunities when they present themselves.

Monotony is a cause of mental fatigue. Doing the same thing day after day is mind numbing. Setting the alarm clock, going to work, coming home, and watching television is like taking a drug. You are able to function, but only at a minimal level.

Many people put their lives on "auto-pilot." They don't think about anything different, don't look for change. They smile at the neighbors and look perfectly normal. However, they have fallen into a life that is so filled with routine that it is virtually the same for 40 or 50 years.

Mental fatigue can also, in many cases, be alleviated with money. Money gives us choices. With money, we can choose to "call in WELL." ("Well, I'm not coming to work today.")

With money, you can take vacations, travel, learn to play an instrument. Money buys you time. The time allows you to exercise your brain muscles. Try it!

Spiritual fatigue—This is the worst, most injurious fatigue. It has many causes, but relatively few manifestations. A person suffering from spiritual fatigue has lost hope. He no longer has a compass to guide his moral convictions.

Losing your faith is a sign of spiritual fatigue. It is marked by cynicism and unhappiness. Perhaps your life has been beset by calamity. Overwhelming misfortune can seemingly be aimed exclusively at you and your family. You feel singled out for unhappiness. You feel forsaken by your family and friends.

I won't claim that money will cure spiritual fatigue. However, there does seem to be one activity that will work. Take your eyes off yourself and start putting God's plan into action by helping others. Of course, this is much easier if you have money!

If a loved one is sick and needs help, wouldn't it be awful if money stands in the way? There is an old saying, "Dig the well BEFORE you need the water." Even if you wait until you need the water, dig the well anyway! Use the well to help and sustain others. It will help you to stop thinking of yourself and to start working for others' needs. It is a sure cure for spiritual fatigue.

What About The Bad Decisions?

So, what do you need to cure your physical, mental, or spiritual fatigue? Shake up your life! Dare to make some decisions! Don't be afraid to make some bad ones!

If you are not making some bad decisions, you are not making enough decisions! You can't simply start out making good decisions. That takes practice. How do you practice? You start making decisions right away. Some of them will be bad. That's okay. You won't get good at making decisions until you get some bad ones out of your system.

Decide—And Choose

Would you like to have more choices in your life? Do you want to choose where you live, where your children attend school, and how often to travel and take vacations? Would you agree with me that these choices will reduce stress, increase your vigor, and make life more interesting? Then make some bad decisions!

It has been said, "Not to decide is to decide." In other words, if you do not make a decision, then you are actually making a decision to do nothing. You are deciding not to change.

You can choose whether to take action, make commitments, and make changes. It is up to you. It all depends on your willingness to make decisions.

When Will Bad Decisions Become Good Decisions?

Your bad decisions will NEVER become good decisions unless you evaluate them against a goal. Your dream will drive your decisions. Any decisions that help you achieve your dream are good ones. Anything that keeps you from the attainment of your dream is bad.

You can learn, either through trial and error or through the teachings of successful people, how to improve your decisions. Over time, you will adjust your actions. Your decisions will get better and better. If your dream is worthwhile, and if you are truly committed to attaining it, your decisions will quickly improve.

Soon, you will be achieving things you never thought possible. Your fatigue will vanish. Your physical, mental, and spiritual well-being will prosper, as your actions and commitment drive you toward higher values. You will be designing your destiny.

As long as we learn from our mistakes, we can grow. As long as we act with integrity and honesty, our mistakes should not have lasting effects on us or our loved ones.

So, make a decision right now. Go ahead, you can do it!

A Personal Note

I have often heard "It is easier to ask for forgiveness than to ask for permission." I believe this is true. I have met too many people who are paralyzed by the fear of making a bad decision. It is not actually being wrong that frightens them. Rather, they are afraid of the consequences.

We worry about what other people will think or say. But aren't these fears often exaggerated? I would know, I have done it. I have personally avoided decisions to act in a responsible manner because I spent too much time imagining the results of making a bad decision. But I have changed!

(continued on next page)

Two things have helped. First, my dreams are much bigger today than they ever were before. I want some things so much that I no longer fear looking foolish—instead I fear not achieving my dreams. Second, I try not to think about what others will think. I do what a man should do in this life.

I am certainly not perfect. There are times I still make many bad decisions. So what? That just shows that I'm on the move!

10 RULES to MAKE

Rule Number 6

Develop X-ray Vision

---

*Never look down to test the ground
before taking your next step:
only he who keeps his eye fixed on the far horizon
will find his right road.*
—Dag Hammarskjold

In 1915, the British and the Turks were involved in a terrible war. A fierce naval battle was being fought, and the British were taking a terrible beating. Finally, the British withdrew. They could not stand any more. Their decision seemed very prudent at the time.

Later, it was learned that at the very moment the British ships turned, the Turks were about to unfurl a white flag of surrender. The Turks were out of ammunition. Their losses were high. Yet, before they could surrender, the battle ended in their favor.

The war continued, with the loss of many thousands more British and Turkish soldiers. Had the British commander simply kept fighting, he would have won the day and the war.

There is a clear lesson to be learned from this example. Develop X-ray vision. Develop the ability to see through the challenges that confront you.

Two Examples Of X-ray Vision

Thomas Alva Edison, the great American inventor, is certainly a man who could look through obstacles and challenges. He collected many patents in his career. He invented everything from the movie projector to the phonograph. But he is best known for the electric light.

The story of this invention is remarkable. Edison, like many others of his day, was searching for a way to harness electric current to replace gas lamps, fireplaces, and candles. Yet, he alone was able to solve the mystery.

The problem was that he needed to develop a filament that would last a long time in the light bulb. Every known fiber of the day was tried. None worked. In fact, Edison experimented with more than 800 different filaments before achieving success.

Imagine, more than 800 filaments. He never quit. The most amazing part was that Edison could only work in the daytime! After all, he had not yet invented the electric light!

There were two tremendous obstacles that Edison faced. First, no one actually knew that an electric light could work. Second, the daunting chore of trying filament after filament was utterly exhausting. He did not know how many trials he would have to make. He just kept on going.

Let's look at these two factors. Each holds a world of motivation for any person interested in creating wealth.

What Did A Light Bulb Look Like?

Imagine the creative process that this man endured to produce his invention. Remember, nothing even remotely like an electric light bulb existed at the time. Edison had to picture it in his mind. He had to create an idea of what he wanted with absolutely no reference points. He needed incredible vision.

But don't forget, he wasn't trying to create a light bulb, he was trying to beat back the darkness. He wanted light! We tend to forget that. He wanted to be able to read at night. His mission was clear. He knew that if he could accomplish this task, the service to mankind would be overwhelming.

Edison had X-ray vision. He could look through the challenges and see the results. In many respects, he is like the man who buys the shovel. The man doesn't want a shovel—he wants to put a hole in the ground.

Do you think if he simply wanted to invent something he would have chosen anything as daunting as a light bulb? Probably not. He could have modified an existing piece of equipment. Instead, because of his X-ray vision, he reshaped the world.

How Many Times Should You Try?

Now, consider the 800 filaments Edison tried before coming up with an answer. Imagine, 800 filaments! How many did he expect to try? Did he set out with a limit? I doubt it. Imagine if he had said, "Well, I'm willing to spend a week on this project," or "I'll try a dozen different filaments. But if I don't get any positive results, I'll call it quits."

If Edison had placed limits on the EFFORT, rather than the result, the light bulb may have been invented much later. He had X-ray vision. He could see the results of the thing he was doing. He could see THROUGH the challenges. His life was not consumed by counting the number of failures he had. They were irrelevant. He was willing to count only the SUCCESSES.

A Revolutionary Idea

More than 150 years before Thomas Edison bathed the world in electric light, a group of American colonists ignited the light of freedom. The British rulers were robbing them of their rights and liberty. The American revolutionaries knew they didn't want to be treated as second-class citizens.

But the king did not grant basic liberties to the colonists. So, this country was invented by men and women who could visualize what it would be like to be free. They didn't think about settling for anything less. They had X-ray vision. When obstacles presented themselves, the colonials had the ability to look through them to the result.

They did not know if democracy would work, for there were no democracies at the time. They did not know how long it would take, how many lives would be lost. They only knew that they HAD TO HAVE THEIR FREEDOM.

Look Through It To The Results

What can you look through with your X-ray vision? Almost anything. Obstacles, challenges, problems, fears, excuses, criticism. Anything. What are the things in your life, in your job, that need your X-ray vision?

With X-ray vision, all obstacles are transparent. That's right. You can see right through them. However, most people don't look through obstacles. They focus on the thing right in front of them. Instead of looking through to the results, their eyesight is limited to the very first thing they see. That is why so many people are unable to overcome the simplest obstacles.

Most excuses are based on fear. Look through the excuse to find the underlying fear someone has. Usually it boils down to a fear of failure. People refuse to take action because it places them in a position where they might suffer ridicule. Help them to see through the fear. Keep them focused on the results.

Whatever It Takes

What should you do once you have developed your X-ray vision? The answer is very simple: DO WHATEVER IT TAKES!

When a chicken is placed in front of a chain link fence, with a bowl of food on the other side, it will run back and forth, squawking and cackling. It can see the food, but cannot figure out how to get to it.

When a dog sees food on the other side of the same fence, he will go AROUND the fence. He might dig UNDER the fence. He might even jump onto a box, a pile of wood, or whatever, and go OVER the fence. He does whatever it takes, and works out a solution.

What kind of animal are you? Will you squawk and cackle, or will you go around, over, or under the obstacle to get what you want?

Determination and commitment, coupled with imagination and daring, will accomplish almost anything.

People who are willing to simply do whatever it takes to reach their goals are leaders worth following. Look to them for inspiration. Become one of them.

More Heroes

Helen Keller lost her hearing and sight in infancy. Yet, during her life, she developed a vision that was truly outstanding. Not only did she grow personally, becoming a woman of letters and a great teacher, she also shared her gift. Were there obstacles? They were so numerous that it is almost mind boggling. Did she succumb to them? Never. She had X-ray vision into the life that seeing and hearing people live.

Imagine the Wright brothers. They had the audacity to believe that man could fly! They could SEE it. How many trials did they have? Were they worthwhile contributors to this planet? There is no question about it.

All You Have To Do Is Follow

Unlike Thomas Edison, your path is already lit. All you have to do is follow the example of successful people. You should design your own destiny, but you can follow the road paved by people who have already achieved what you want to achieve.

Isn't that a lot less challenging than inventing the light bulb, the airplane, or a whole new form of government? Absolutely. All you have to do is to overcome a few personal fears.

How often do you need to do things that others are not willing to do? How many challenges, obstacles, excuses, and criticisms must you look through on the way to your ultimate goal?

It doesn't matter! It just doesn't matter! Do whatever it takes to reach your success. Develop X-ray vision!

A Personal Note

I have a plaque on my wall that was given to me after a speech I made. It has a photograph of a skier standing at the top of a very steep slope. On the slope are huge moguls (mounds of snow). It is a daunting scene.

Across the bottom of the plaque are these words: "Obstacles are the scary things you see when you take your eyes off your
(continued on next page)

---

goals." This plaque was the inspiration for this rule to make, *Develop X-ray Vision*. It is so true. If you focus on the challenges instead of looking through to the goals, the impact is very frightening, and may stop you in your tracks. Keep your eyes on your goals, and, once you've attained them, you'll hardly remember the challenges you've overcome.

10 RULES to MAKE

Rule Number 7

You Are Who Your Friends Are

Chance makes our parents, but choice makes our friends.
—Jacques Delille

There is a story about a man who walked into a bar and sat down. He noticed the fellow sitting next to him and exclaimed, "Excuse me, are you Irish?"
"Why, yes I am," replied the second man.
"That's terrific," said the first. "So am I!"
"What County in Ireland are you from?" asked the second.
"County Cork," replied the first.
"What an incredible coincidence," said the second. "So am I."
"Glory be," came the response, "that is a coincidence. What town in Cork?"
"You probably never heard of it. 'Tis a tiny place called Middletown."
"Saints preserve us. That is exactly where I was born."
"You have GOT to be kidding me. What street were you born on?"
"Main street."
"This is too much. I was born on Main street. I lived there for many years."
"What year were you born?"
"1959."
"This is unbelievable. So was I!"

A stranger, overhearing the conversation, asked the bartender what was going on. "Oh," said the bartender, "it's just the O'Leary twins. Pay them no mind."

This silly story serves to remind us that we can't choose our families. Whether we like it or not, whether we live in the same town or move half way around the world, our relatives will always be our relatives.

We can, however, choose our friends. In this world, you'd best choose your friends carefully!

A Bad Crowd

When you were growing up, did your parents warn you against hanging out with a bad crowd? Did you know anyone who was a really good kid; then, all of a sudden, they began to get into trouble? Did they start to hang out with a bad crowd?

We warn our children about the friends they choose. We know the tremendous influence that a group can have. It is difficult to break bonds that are formed through years of association.

Too often we forget the lessons of childhood. We ignore the advice that we so freely give our children. We choose friends who share common interests when we should also look for people who share our values.

There Are Friends And There Are Acquaintances

I am not implying that every single person you associate with should pass some sort of values test. There is a huge difference between your friends and your acquaintances. I have a very good friend named Barry. We do a lot of things together and I really appreciate him. He is an excellent example of a caring individual with great ambition. In fact, he has created a very handsome lifestyle for his family.

Barry and I play golf together. We are often looking for two other people to round out our foursome. For the most part, they are acquaintances. As long as they are good company, that is all we ask. If they have some problems in their personal lives, it is not discussed. I don't look to them for leadership, or as a role model. They are simply people who play golf and whose schedules are convenient.

Barry is a different story. He even introduced me to his publisher and was instrumental in getting my first book published. Being his friend has changed my life for the better. We share values. We have the same convictions.

Barry and I are not clones. We are of different religions, yet we each respect the opinions and views of the other. Although we may disagree on the methods for achieving certain ends, we usually agree on the outcomes we want in life. He is a good man.

Barry is a terrible fisherman, though. Fishing is my ultimate pursuit. I love it. But, going fishing with Barry can be a real trial. In fact, the first time we went together, I asked him to go to the bait store. He decided to take a short cut and went to the pet store instead. He bought some large tropical fish, at a very hefty price. I didn't like using pets for bait.

So, when I am really serious about fishing, I don't go with Barry. I have other friends, and some acquaintances, who are better for fishing. They know how to fish, and that is great. But they aren't my very best friends. I don't look to them for an example. We don't share deep conversations. Instead, we talk about fishing.

The point is that I have many acquaintances, but only a few good friends. I don't get them mixed up. Only my friends have a major influence on my life.

You are probably the same way.

However, even your acquaintances may influence you. If they are negative, then it may make you negative. If they are cheaters, it may hurt you. If they don't obey the law, sooner or later, you may be placed in a compromising position.

It is important to associate with people who have the same fundamental values as you. Even acquaintances should behave in a manner that is consistent with your judgment. Remember, your dear friends will probably develop from the ranks of your acquaintances.

Guilt By Association

A friend of mine is a Mormon. We were at dinner one evening and I ordered a beer. He had a glass of water. "Why don't you try a non-alcoholic beer?" I asked. "They taste great." His reply was very telling. "For us, drinking is immoral. So, we try to avoid even the APPEARANCE of sin." That was a great answer.

Even if you are not guilty of something wrong, if you ASSOCIATE with unsavory, dishonest, or unworthy individuals, you will LOOK guilty. Even the strongest individual is placing himself in danger by associating with the wrong people.

Dexter Yager, the multi-millionaire, super-motivational network marketer, has written a book titled *Don't Let Anyone Steal Your Dreams*. Who is he warning us about? Is it our enemies? Is it the people we most dislike in the world? No, IT MAY BE OUR FRIENDS!

Where Are They Going?

Look at your circle of friends. Where are they going in life? Do they have ambition? Are they looking for opportunities to improve their lives and serve their families? Do they waste their time, or are they using their time to improve their financial position? What kind of people are they?

You need to associate with people who are already successful, or who are working hard to achieve success. It is really very simple. Remember, if you ARE successful, wouldn't it be nice to have some friends left?

Dad And The Lottery

A few years ago, the lottery in Pennsylvania was for more than $100 million. My parents were at a dinner with some of their very good friends. Each person was asked what they would do if they won the money. When it came to my father, he had a story that shocked everyone.

"The first thing I would probably have to do is get some new friends." The sentence fell like a sword in the room. My father is usually rather quiet and an extremely nice person. His friends were silent for a few seconds, then pandemonium broke loose.

"What?" they shouted. "What do you mean? Are you saying we wouldn't be good enough for you if you were rich?"

"It's not that," said my father. "But you wouldn't have enough money to do the things I want to do."

As you can imagine, the rest of the evening was a little tense. Everyone assumed that if one of them suddenly became wealthy, the rest of them would naturally enjoy the money, too. Of course, it wouldn't work that way. My father was right. He would probably need new friends. My father would be able to quit his job, he and my mother could travel when they wanted, stay in fine hotels, and so forth. Who else could join them?

Growing Together, Not Apart

When you were growing up, you and your friends learned lessons together. Each year, you entered a new grade in school. Each year, the lesson plans brought everyone along at roughly the same speed. If you kept pace, you were promoted to the next grade. If you did not, you were kept back.

This was a good system, as it kept everyone in the class progressing at the same speed. Recently, many schools have adopted policies where individuals can progress even faster than the rest of the group. These gifted students aren't allowed to simply go off on their own. They are placed into groups that are also progressing rapidly.

If this system of individual growth is good, why do we abandon it when we get older? All of a sudden, most people stop growing.

We form a group of friends who are all about the same level, and we simply STOP growing! We stop reading, stop writing, and stop communicating about important issues.

We raise our children, have jobs, join the PTA. However, most people do not continue to grow. They find comfort in a group of friends who are basically alike. It becomes very difficult to break out of that mold. If you are the only one who has a dream, then your friends may hold you back.

You Need To Do Two Things

First, develop successful acquaintances. Your friends must be acquaintances first. This is like the minor league for baseball players. It is a training and testing facility. Associate with successful, or at least ambitious, people. Look for people who have what you want to have. Do they have both time and money? Are their values and behaviors admirable and enduring? Are they living, or trying to live, the lifestyle you want?

Second, offer your old friends the opportunity to become successful WITH you. Look for people who are not afraid to change their habits in order to achieve a worthwhile goal. Work together, as a team, to achieve mutual goals.

Positive Plus Positive Equals Success

Please don't think that I am suggesting you go out and dump all your friends. Nor should you give them an ultimatum. The process will be gradual, but it will be certain. As you grow and prosper, your friends who are unwilling to change and grow may slowly disappear. They will not share the same dreams and accept the same challenges that will now fill your life.

Should you stop calling them, associating with them, or caring about them? No, stay in touch. Give them support, understand them, and always love them. Help them when they need it.

Develop a positive, "can do" attitude. Then associate with positive people. This combination is unbelievable. Remember, positive people can turn you into a positive force. A negative person cannot help you become positive. You may feel better in comparison, but you will not move forward.

The choice is yours. Will you create the sum of your life from negative or positive parts? You cannot be any greater than what you put into your heart. Make the parts positive. Meet and befriend positive people. Stack the odds in your favor.

What about your current friends? How should you treat them? Always have a smile for old friends. They are a part of your life, and they are a part of you. Part of what you take forward will be created by them. After all, you are who your friends are!

A Personal Note

I have been blessed with great friends. From my longest lasting friendship with Herb (40 years and still going strong) to some of my newest friends, my life has been full of good people. But I am most fortunate because my very best friend is my wife, Jeanne.

We share interests, dreams, children and values. We are both committed to personal growth that will help us be better friends for each other. We are working together on a business that can help us reach our dreams. I didn't know life could be this good. Now I know it can be.

I hope that you are fortunate enough to find friends like mine.

10 RULES to MAKE

Rule Number 8

Bill's Rule: Show People What's in It for Them

> *Give me that which I want,*
> *and you shall have that which you want.*
> —Adam Smith,
> 18th-century economist

First, let me say that Bill's Rule is an idea that has been professed by many others. It is simply called Bill's Rule because I was the first one to write it down.

Bill's Rule is simple:

No one will consistently do something for you unless you can show them what is in it for them.

That's it. It is not complex. There are no great secrets here. However, it is unquestionably true. Everyone adheres to this rule. They may not admit it, but they do.

Walt Disney's movie *Lady and the Tramp* provides a lesson for anyone who wishes to MAKE the rule *Show People What's in It for Them*.

In the story, Lady has a muzzle put over her snout. She is unable to remove it, and runs away in sadness and disgrace. Her "boyfriend," Tramp, devises an ingenious plan to remove it. He leads her to a pond where a beaver is struggling with a log, trying to pull it into the water.

Tramp asks the beaver if he would like a "log puller" to help in the work. All the beaver has to do is gnaw off the "handy-dandy log puller" modeled by Lady. The beaver quickly nibbles through a strap. Lady is free of the muzzle, and the beaver has his log puller. Everyone is happy, and everyone gets what he wants.

The moral to this story is easy. If you expect people to do something for you, you must show them what's in it for them!

Is This Rule Cynical?

Some people will claim that they do things without expecting a reward. Your parents, for example, will sacrifice almost anything for you. My wife and I will do almost anything for our children. We do not expect a reward. But you know what? We get one.

We receive love from our children. We get the satisfaction of knowing that we provide for them. We do our very best as parents, and that is all the reward we need. But make no mistake, there is a reward there.

Are there people in your life who seem to do things for you without expecting anything in return? Well, there is something for these people. They may derive satisfaction from the smile on your face. They may feel responsible for you and will attempt to satisfy their feelings by helping you. They may believe that they owe a past debt to your family. In any event, these people will still get something by helping you. You may never know what it is, but it will be very real to the other people.

However, most people need something more tangible in order to *consistently* do something for you. They need to establish a feeling of equity. That is, they want to get something in return for the things they do.

Some people have a hard time relating to this. They feel it is cynical. Well, it isn't. This is how people operate. There is absolutely nothing wrong with it. In fact, anyone who does something for you DESERVES, and is ENTITLED to, something in return. It is more than a rule, it is a law of human nature.

So, give things to other people. It may not be money or goods, it could simply be appreciation. Whatever it is, it should be equal to, or exceed, the value of what you received.

A Question Of Consistency

Look at Bill's Rule again. Notice the words "No one will CONSISTENTLY do something for you." The key word here is "consistently." We want to create a consistent stream of mutually favorable activities between ourselves and those around us. Consistency means that we have a dependable set of actions. We can begin to trust the other person.

This idea of building trust through consistent behavior extends to all human relationships. Trust is fundamental. You cannot trust someone who has erratic behavior. It makes it too difficult to let down your guard. You become unwilling to engage in supportive activities with the other person because you never know how he will react. You have no trust, and the relationship falters.

In business, trust is important. With trust comes a chance for the relationship to grow. This growth can promote mutually agreeable activities that benefit both parties.

So, let's get back to Bill's Rule. We want to show people how they will benefit so that they will do things for us. That's it.

Always show people what is in it for them. Unless they realize they will receive consistent rewards for helping you, they will soon stop doing it.

A Question Of What Is Important

Don't forget that the operative words here are "... unless you can show them what's in it for *them*." Don't show them what is in it for *you*. Show them what's in it for *them*. In order to do this, you must know what they want.

What Do People Want?

Unfortunately, many people are unable to tell you what they want. There are two main reasons. First, they might be embarrassed that you think they want something. We have been taught that it is not polite to expect something for doing a good deed for someone else. There are a lot of people who feel like this. They have not yet learned how people are motivated.

The second reason for people not being able to tell you what they want is that they do not KNOW what they want. They have not built a dream, set goals, or taken a course of action that will help them reach those goals! Without a goal, they will not have consistent behavior.

This is not to say that you should avoid these people. Help them. Teach them to dream and to strive consistently for their goals. This is especially important if these people are already part of your life. Parents, children, spouses, and others can learn to love, trust, achieve, and grow through your example and help.

Once someone DOES know what they want, find out what it is. Make sure that they feel it is important enough to put out some effort to get it.

A Question Of Equity

When someone asks himself, *What's in It for Me?* he is also saying, "Is the reward at least EQUAL to the expected work or effort?" This idea of equity is extremely important. It symbolizes the real essence of Bill's Rule. If there is no perceived equity, the other person will soon lose interest in doing something for you.

How can you determine equity? You can't. "What?" you say. "I can't DETERMINE what's equitable for the other person? Then how can I give him something that is equal to his effort?"

The reason YOU cannot determine what is equitable for another person is that HE is the only one who can assess equity for himself. This principle is violated so often it is almost astonishing. People are constantly deciding what THEY think is equitable for OTHER people.

One major problem is that we always want more. Always? Yes, always. When we receive something for our effort, we tend to build an image of equity. For example, on a job, most people feel that they are underpaid. At the very least, they feel that they receive the bare minimum of a fair exchange. Very few people go around with the idea that they are overpaid.

When we get a raise, does it make the equity factor change? No. Why? The answer is quite simple. Most people get a raise for work they have already done! Did you realize that? You have already put in the extra effort. You have already stayed later, worked harder, developed more expertise. You don't get a raise for work you are ABOUT to do.

When I first thought about this, after reading the book *The Equity Factor* by Richard Huseman, I started to laugh out loud. This is so true! Yet, we almost always forget it. People who have already done something will not see their rewards as an incentive, they will see them as just payment for what they have already done. So, if we want to motivate someone, we must, in effect, PROMISE him something.

This is why Bill's Rule is structured the way it is. We only ask people to do something if we can show them "What's in it for them." We will not tell them afterward—that's simply a payment for work already done! We will tell them ahead of time. This motivates them! And, if we structure it right, we will let them get more and more and more and more...without a ceiling or end to the reward.

Why Giving Is The Best Policy

This is the ultimate message of Bill's Rule. Don't be afraid to give more and more. The reason: because people WANT more and more. They do. And that is all right. It is natural. More importantly, they deserve it.

If you expect people to do things for you, you must show them what they will gain by doing it. You must structure it so there is no limit to what they can attain. It's that simple.

A Personal Note

As I write this particular section, I really get fired up! I want you to understand the importance of showing people what's in it for them. It has absolutely changed my life. By taking the time to learn what people want, I have become a better friend, husband, parent, partner, and leader. I hope these pages will bring you the same results.

I hesitate to call this Bill's Rule because it is not just mine. Someone taught it to me. If you like, rename this rule after yourself. It doesn't matter what you call it, just use it. Base your relationships on giving other people what they want. They will give you love, trust, and help in return.

---

10 RULES to MAKE

Rule Number 9

Go a Little Crazy

*If you would hit the mark,
you must aim a little above it.
Every arrow that flies feels the attraction of the earth.*
—Henry Wadsworth Longfellow

In 1992, Southwest Airlines faced a high-stakes dilemma. Its much advertised slogan, "Just Plane Smart," was unfortunately too similar to the "Plane Smart" logo already being used by Stevens Aviation, an airline sales company in South Carolina. It seemed that a lawsuit was imminent.

But a lawsuit is how ordinary people settle their business differences. Herb Kelleher, Southwest's crazy-like-a-fox CEO, is no ordinary person. Along with the CEO of Stevens Aviation, he staged "Malice in Dallas." The two men actually agreed to arm wrestle for the right to use the slogan! The newspapers and television journalists jumped on the story, giving each company enormous publicity.

Amid much fanfare and ballyhoo, Southwest's Kelleher lost the struggle. With the crowd cheering and chanting, he was carried off in a stretcher. And what about the "Plane Smart" trademark? Stevens Aviation agreed to let

Southwest Airlines use it anyway. By going a little crazy, both companies had received such great, positive publicity that the details really didn't matter.

How does this story apply to you? It's simple: *Go a Little Crazy.* Don't get stuck in the same old traps that hold so many people back. If these two companies had used the courts to settle their disputes, the only people to profit would have been the lawyers. Are you brave enough to go a little crazy? I hope so. You *need to do it!*

How Crazy Should You Be?

You should be as crazy as you need to be in order to achieve your dreams. It is that simple. Don't try to analyze it too much. Just go with it.

A while back, I read a great story in *Reader's Digest.* One part of the story stands out clearly and has helped me in building relationships with many people.

The author was once boarding a cruise ship. Ahead of him, in the long line of passengers, was a very slow-moving woman in her eighties. She shuffled along all by herself until, suddenly, the band struck up a lively tune. The old woman straightened up and did a little dance. She hopped around and went a little crazy!

The author made a great point about this woman's behavior. His theory was that she did not view herself as an old woman. She still saw herself as the young girl who had once performed a lively dance whenever she heard music. The tune on the boat rekindled her vision of herself and released the young girl within her once more.

Was she crazy? If you saw that woman do a little dance in the middle of the street would you move across to the other side? In her mind, she was simply behaving as the young girl she remembered.

This is an important point to remember. None of us see ourselves as others see us. We are still our parents' child, the young adult in the prime of life. All of us have a vigorous, energetic, and spirited person living within the walls of our body. Most other people don't view us that way. They see only the facade: the gray hair, the wrinkles, the job status, and such. They don't see our inner, crazier, FREE self.

If this is true, then we also may not see the free spirit in others. We often do not want to see it. We feel safer if everyone is a little reserved. We want them to be quiet, steady, and secure.

Mere Child's Play

Children are a little crazy. I have two lovely girls under the age of seven. They are both free spirits. Thank God for that! Wouldn't it be awful if they acted as I do? They wouldn't be children. They want to go out in the rain, not hide inside. Every meal is a new adventure for them. They EXPLORE their food, marvel at it. Ice cream isn't something they eat to overcome their disappointments, it is a celebration!

They wake up every morning with great excitement. Each day holds so much promise. The simplest things bring them so much pleasure. When they are sad or unhappy, it is so easy to turn those feelings into joy. Their tears end with a smile and a laugh. Is that crazy?

The craziness and enthusiasm of children is infectious. Not only do my kids get their friends excited about the most mundane events, they get ME all fired up as well. Conversely, I have re-learned how to speak and play with children. We don't need organized sports or big events. We simply let our imaginations carry us away. In short, we go a little crazy.

Children are not bound by status. They have nothing to prove. They accept each other for what they are: a playmate, a friend, or a loving influence. They don't notice the clothes, the cars, or the houses. They only see the fun and the interesting oddities that fill their world with opportunities.

So What Happened?

How do we lose the ability to act a little crazy? We allow the day-to-day reality to overcome our natural abilities. Instead of acting a little crazy, we begin to act a little serious. When that gets rewarded, we start to act a lot serious.` Finally, we can't help ourselves. We are bound by status and expectations.

But this is important: The rewards we can get from acting a little crazy are far more abundant than the rewards for holding back our inner selves.

In order to be able to act a little crazy, we must put ourselves in a position where this will be rewarded. Imagine walking into your office on Monday morning, making a chain out of paper clips, and putting them on your head like a halo. What would happen? Is it likely that your boss would do the same thing? Or would he call security and have you removed?

Or try this. Get some of your colleagues together and put some music on the office system. Stand on your chair and lead them in a song. Get them to cheer, clap, and chant. It should be easy, right?

We act like we think we SHOULD act, not how we would really like to act. GET RID OF THAT BEHAVIOR. GO A LITTLE CRAZY. Your financial future depends on it. You have to be a little different to think you can have more than almost anyone you know.

Get Fired Up

I have learned a lot over the past few years by observing some master wealth creators in the network marketing business. If you have never been to a major network marketing event, you have missed out on a terrific experience.

I once attended a function where the participants were singing and dancing in the aisles. There were about 2,000 people there, all having fun. Well, not quite all of them. Some people, me included, were a little reluctant to let go. After all, we had status. We couldn't act like that.

The problem is, status is a prison. It prevents us from showing enthusiasm and excitement. We cannot truly enjoy life because we are too worried about how we might look to others.

At one particular network marketing function, I couldn't help but notice that the very successful speaker did not worry about status. He simply wanted to be wealthy so that he could have fun and help others. In fact, he BECAME wealthy by having fun and helping others.

The speaker pointed out that some people probably didn't feel comfortable with the excitement, the singing, and the cheering. After all, this was a business meeting. (I felt like he was looking right at me when he said this, even though I was trying to act inconspicuous. "Status," you understand.)

He then proceeded to explain that his business was based on excitement and innovation. It was impossible to get others excited unless you were excited. He wondered, and now I do as well, why people feel comfortable acting VERY crazy at football games, yet they are not willing to act a LITTLE crazy at a business meeting where they can become financially free. He made a great point.

The Only Limitations You Have Are Those You Put On Yourself

The moral here is clear. You can choose to adhere to rigorous social standards and business customs, creating perceived "status" for yourself. Or you can go a little crazy and become wealthy. There are people who are waiting to follow your lead.

Remember, they have that child inside them. The business executive in the suit still views himself as the young man who ran and jumped and played. The mother of three still views herself as the young girl who had no worries. Bring it back for them.

But first, bring it back for yourself. You deserve the opportunity to let out the child, the teenager, or the young adult. Remember the vigor, the curiosity and the unparalleled fun you had.

Of course, make sure you have a system that will reward you for the fun you are having.

Commitment And Passion

Almost any worthwhile pursuit will require your enthusiastic and unbridled commitment in order to succeed. It really doesn't matter what it is.

Throw yourself into your pursuit. Become a passionate supporter of those who help you succeed. Let your NATURAL instincts for fun and adventure drive your spirit. Don't be bound by the conventions that EVERYONE ELSE is trying to place on you. While it may seem that they want you to be just like them, some of them are secretly hoping that you will show them a better, more exuberant, way to live. Not everyone will follow you, but enough people will to make you wealthy!

Can you do it? Can you throw yourself into something worthwhile with an abandon necessary to see it through to its ultimate goal? Do you have the personal will, the friendship of great leaders, and the blessings of God to soar with the eagles?

You do! Let it out! Have a blast!

A Personal Note

I used to be a "numbers guy." I didn't want to hear about emotions. Just give me the facts, the numbers. I thought
(continued on next page)

everyone else was the same way. Then I read *Personality Plus* by Florence Littauer. What a revelation!

I discovered that, instead of everyone being like me, only about five percent of the people in the United States are numbers guys like me. And those five percent are dull! Don't get me wrong, I love a sense of humor, singing, and dancing. (After all, I am Irish.) But I had focused all my attention on proving or disproving things, not SHOUTING about them.

Today, I am a child in training. I am learning what it is like to have fun while making money and achieving my dreams. I am learning how to share that excitement with others. I am learning how to let go of my status and do what is best for my family.

If I can do it, you can too. *Go a Little Crazy!*

10 RULES to MAKE

Rule Number 10

Enjoy the Journey

---

*I've learned that people are in such a hurry
to get to the "good life" that they often
rush right past it.*
—A 72-year-old, as quoted by
H. Jackson Brown, Jr.

The following story is borrowed from the famous Irish comedian Hal Roach:

A man was attempting to cross the Atlantic Ocean in a hot air balloon. He left the United States and started out on the treacherous journey. All he could think about was how great it would be when he reached the European continent. He kept himself alert by picturing the wonderful reception he would receive, the riches he would accrue through sponsorships, and the fame he would enjoy.

Finally, after two weeks in the sky, he spotted land. He let some air out of the balloon and descended to within 50 feet of the ground. Although he did not know it, he was hovering over Ireland. He saw a farmer out in his fields and called out to him, "Where am I?" The old Irish farmer looked up at the balloonist and shouted back, "You can't fool me, you're up there in that little basket!"

This story reminds us of a very simple lesson. It is important to enjoy the journey, as well as the goal. The balloonist was so concerned with making it to his final destination that he forgot to enjoy the ride. Instead of looking out on the scenery, he only wanted to get the trip over.

Where Are You Looking? Be A Visionary!

It is absolutely essential to set goals and to create dreams. This book contains many discussions about this process. However, there is a great deal to be enjoyed while accomplishing goals and dreams.

The question is "Where should you look?" It is important to look in all directions: ahead, side to side, down, and back. Only by looking and appreciating all of the beauty, fun, and excitement of our world can we achieve the greatest degree of satisfaction.

Let's take a moment to discuss ways to look at the world—ahead, side to side, down, and back.

Look Ahead

We MUST establish clear, dramatic, and rewarding dreams and goals. And we must enjoy visualizing our dreams and goals.

We must also reinforce the dreams of others. It is really exciting to learn what motivates those who are most important to you. For example, if your wife really wants to quit her job and stay home full time with the kids, encourage her to take a day off and plan some time with the children. Get a movie schedule for them. Call the local library and make a list of the reading sessions and story times. If your husband wants to sharpen his golf game, sign him up for some lessons. Schedule his lesson for a weekday. (It's much less crowded!)

For your friends who like to travel, cut out articles from magazines or the newspaper. Send them the articles with a short note. Rent travel videos for them and keep them excited.

Share your own dreams and do "dream-building sessions." Take a friend or your spouse to the marina, the imported car lot, or the lobby of a resort hotel, and talk about your dreams. In other words—you can design your destiny and have a great time in the process!

Looking Side To Side

It is very important to keep your eyes on your goals. However, you will miss a lot of fun along the way if you do not look around. I call it looking from side to side. Here is the most important aspect of looking from side to side: You will discover other people who are on the same journey as you!

It's easy to feel alone when you have a strong dream. It sometimes seems like you are the only one pursuing this course of action. Sure, there are lots of people who are just standing still—not reaching for their dreams. On the other hand, there are many lovely people who also have developed tunnel vision. They could be standing right next to you, focused on the same goals. However, if they aren't looking from side to side, they will miss you.

Be the one who breaks the ice and looks for others. You will begin to form strong associations that will last a lifetime. You can share your triumphs and tragedies with these fellow travelers—but only if you look for them.

Professional associations, conventions, and other gathering places for like-minded people offer an excellent opportunity for side-to-side viewing and enjoyment.

So, look from side to side. You'll discover that you are not alone. Your world is full of people with the same ideas that motivate you. Share some time with them!

Look Down

While looking from side to side will uncover the PEOPLE in your life, looking down will show you where you are and why you should enjoy it. If you can look down and see a new view, then you are on your way up, and that is exciting.

One of the great joys of looking down is recognizing that you are here and not somewhere else. Too often we are so focused on the future, on our dreams, that we miss the opportunities to really appreciate our present good fortune. This is incredibly easy to do. It is absolutely frightening that we take so much for granted.

If you are unhappy with your present condition, look at the alternatives: You could be homeless, poverty stricken, in jail, sick, or worse!

Now, what about enjoying the things you do have? Consider family, friends, health, home, time, vacations, and the like. Don't take these things for granted. You earned them through toil and attention, didn't you?

Perhaps your home is not as big as you would like. Perhaps it is not located on the water, with a boat at the dock. On the other hand, remember the excitement you felt when you first purchased this property? Reclaim it for yourself. Savor it. You earned it.

Look down and smile.

Look Back

If you are like most of us, you planned your life based on the advice of parents and teachers. They said to get a good job, stick with it, and move up the ladder, and you would have all the things you wanted. You soon learned that this was true—as long as you didn't want security, lifestyle, and freedom.

However, you probably have been making steady advances. Look back on the accomplishments of your life. How far have you come? How many lives have you touched? Remember, you are not making this journey alone. You influence many people along the way. What would the world be like without your special input?

For a great reminder of the effect you have on others, see the movie *It's A Wonderful Life*, starring Jimmy Stewart. In this classic film, Stewart wishes that he had never been born. A friendly angel named Clarence grants him his wish. When Stewart returns to his home town, neighbors and loved ones are quite different. People who were helped by Stewart in his original life had fallen on bad times. His children were never born.

What effects have you had on the lives of other people? You have surely made a difference. Your whole life is a journey to be savored. Don't get lost in the past. Don't let it haunt you or hold you back. *DO* view it as a worthwhile endeavor that has made a difference.

Remember, life is made up of choices. Your position in life today is determined by the choices you made years ago. It will take time to change your situation, because your choices today will not bear fruit for some time. Don't overlook the accomplishments gained through your hard work.

A Personal Note

I love re-reading this chapter. It always makes me feel good about myself and my accomplishments so far. It is so easy to lose sight of those accomplishments. As Jeanne and I strive to achieve our dreams and goals, we must CONSTANTLY and CONSCIOUSLY tell each other that we are proud of our lives—and that we have already made a difference.

(continued on next page)

I have gotten a lot better at looking around for other people who are on the journey. You are one of those people. I am happy that we have connected through this book. If you have read this far, you are certainly a person who is on the journey to success. I am honored to be traveling with you.

Conclusion

A Vision for My Destiny

Conclusion

A Vision for My Destiny

It is another one of those perfect summer days—just as it was at the opening of this book. But it is not 1993, it's 25 years in the future. Now, instead of sitting on the dock, I am on MY yacht, with MY family. The same warm sun is shining. The same salty, fragrant air wafts over the water in a warming embrace. Everything is the same as the scene in 1993—except for the fates of Jeanne, our daughters, and me.

I am sitting in the stern, holding my grandson on my lap. My daughter Amanda and her husband are standing in the doorway to the main cabin. The air conditioning drifts through the opening, cooling them after a long day on the water.

"I can't tell if your dad is smiling or crying," says my son-in-law. "It looks like he's doing both." Amanda turns to look at her son and me. "He's always a little teary-eyed when we pass this dock," says Amanda. "This is were it all began for him."

My family walks over and surrounds me with their love and their presence. We have had the journey of a lifetime. Jeanne, Amanda, Kathleen, and their families know that this is where the decision was made.

This is the place where I regained my dream. This is the place where I made the decision to break outdated rules and to search for new, creative rules that allowed me to design my own destiny.

"Are we going to say the words again?" asks my grandson.

"We have to say them," I remind him. "We only achieve our dreams by encouraging others."

As the sun settled below the horizon, the calm and quiet lent a peace that is only found on the water. It was time for our family ritual.

We turned toward the people on the dock, people we did not know but who deserved our help, and raised our voices in unison:

"Design Your Destiny!"

Some people will.

Some people won't.

How about you?